Dr. Saul Miller is a clinical psychologist and a graduate of McGill University and the Institute of Psychiatry, University of London, England. He is a clinician, a researcher, and a teacher. His collaborator, Dr. Jo Anne Miller, is a social psychologist and a graduate of McGill University and the London School of Economics and Political Science. For the past fifteen years the Millers have lived and worked throughout North America, Europe, and Asia.

PRENTICE-HALL, INC.
Englewood Cliffs, New Jersey 07632

A SPECTRUM BOOK

SAUL MILLER
with Jo Anne Miller

FOOD
FOR
THOUGHT

A NEW LOOK AT
FOOD & BEHAVIOR

Library of Congress Cataloging in Publication Data

MILLER, SAUL.
  Food for thought.

  (A Spectrum Book)
  Includes bibliographical references and index.
    1. Nutrition.   2. Human behavior—Nutritional
aspects.   3. Nutritionally induced diseases.
4. Food habits.   I. Miller, Jo Anne, joint author.
II. Title.
QP141.M436   613.2   79-21159
ISBN 0-13-322842-8
ISBN 0-13-322834-7 pbk.

Editorial/production supervision by Carol Smith
Cover design by Judith Kazdym Leeds
Manufacturing buyer: Cathie Lenard

A SPECTRUM BOOK

Printed in the United States of America

10   9   8   7   6   5   4   3   2   1

PRENTICE-HALL INTERNATIONAL, INC., *London*
PRENTICE-HALL OF AUSTRALIA, PTY. LIMITED, *Sydney*
PRENTICE-HALL OF CANADA, LTD., *Toronto*
PRENTICE-HALL OF INDIA PRIVATE LIMITED, *New Delhi*
PRENTICE-HALL OF JAPAN, INC., *Tokyo*
PRENTICE-HALL OF SOUTHEAST ASIA PTE. LTD., *Singapore*
WHITEHALL BOOKS LIMITED, *Wellington, New Zealand*

To Jonathan

Many people contributed to *Food for Thought*. I especially wish to acknowledge my collaborator and wife, Dr. Jo Anne Miller. I also wish to express my gratitude to my parents, Morris and Anne Miller, and to Michio Kushi, the Sams family, Sharon and Paul Wolfe, Dr. Abram Hoffer, Dr. John Prince, Lucinda Vardey, Joseph and Anne Wawrykow, Lynne Lumsden, Carol Smith, Dr. L.M. McEwen, Dennis Hayes, Tony Naegle, N. Pritikin, Betty Shepherd, Hugh Pearson, Yoshio Kawahara, Dr. A. Rabinovitch, The East West Foundation, The Canada Council, The Sivananda Yoga Association, those whose writings influenced this work, and all those friends and colleagues throughout the world who extended their hospitality and shared their experience.

Contents

It is a pleasure to welcome this fine book to the growing literature on good nutrition, for only the education of the public about the connection between good food and good health will begin to counteract the massive increase in disease for which our culture is noted.

The author outlines a unique scheme for classifying what we eat along a one-dimensional continuum. Substances too rich in unnatural food constituents such as sugar and alcohol are at one end of the continuum (the expansive), while substances too rich in protein are at the other, the constrictive, end. The foods in the middle are the central foods. These are the ones which are whole, natural and not mutilated by man. The extremes include food artifacts, junk or garbage foods. They are the products of man's manipulation of food.

It is refreshing to have a book on nutrition which deals with the health-producing properties of food rather than with their chemical classification into the main food constituents. This must be easier to

Foreword

understand and follow for most people. People interested in eating to become and remain well want to know how they can do so in their selection of food, not in the selection of food artifacts such as protein, fat or carbohydrate. The chemist's way of looking at food simply turns off the average person, and rightly so.

The author suggests that expansive foods create expansive personalities or habits, while constrictive foods tend to cause constrictive personalities. In general, my observations over twenty-eight years of psychiatry support this idea.

Another interesting idea is the law of opposites. A moment's reflection suggests why this is a natural law. All we have to assume is that the body has a need for a quantity of protein which, when met, turns off our interest in more protein. A diet very rich in meat, a protein-rich food, will require substances rich in calories but low in protein, in order to meet this natural desire to decrease protein intake. Conversely, a diet high in sugar will create a need for foods high in protein. Our national diet with an annual consumption of 240 pounds of protein and 120 pounds of sugar per person per year illustrates the law of opposites. The solution is to eat primarily the central foods which, of course, are free of junk.

Each cell of our body lives within a chemical environment with which it exchanges molecules, absorbing what it requires and releasing what it no longer needs. If this environment fails to contain adequate numbers of essential molecules, the cells will not function as well. In the same way, a bricklayer with no bricks around will not be able to build. This internal environment is fed by our external environment—by what we eat, drink and breathe.

If we allow harmful molecules to enter the internal cellular environment we will create problems for our cells which may not be solvable by the cells. When this happens we become ill, metabolically sick. If continued over a long period we will develop any one or more of a large variety of diseases ranging from psychiatric diseases to most of the chronic physical degenerative diseases. Should we not, then, treat our cells with respect and careful attention?

This book provides a useful prescription or formula for ensuring that our internal environment will be optimum for our cells. I have gone over this book very carefully and have concluded that it will harm no one and will help nearly everyone who follows its principles, for it takes into account the principles of variability and individuality as well as ensuring that the best information we have, now called orthomolecular nutrition, will be incorporated into this way of eating.

A. Hoffer, M.D., Ph.D.

This is a new and different book about food and behavior. It describes how the food we eat can affect what we think, say, and do...and suggests how to eat to increase our well-being and pleasure.

The book is unique for several reasons.

- It discusses food as we know it and talk about it: as bread, cheese, apples, steak, salad, chocolate—not as nutritional concepts (calories, minerals, vitamins) which can be confusing and which put the intuition to sleep.
- Similarly, it discusses behavior in terms of aggression, violence, dependence, sex and learning problems—not as psychological concepts which are difficult to understand or relate to.

Preface

• It is not a diet book. Instead, it describes the principles and *dynamics* of sane eating in such a way that readers can learn *for themselves* how to balance their food...and their lifestyle.

Food for Thought is for everyone interested in improving the quality of life as well as for the entire "health conscious" market. It deals with issues of broad interest: sanity, sexuality, stress and attractiveness. It explains why eating meat leads to a craving for sweets, why you won't permanently lose weight and feel satisfied on a "high-protein diet" and how to eat to reduce tension and stress. It includes whatever psychological data are available; however, it focuses more on personal experience and observation, anecdote and case study, making it very readable.

A NOTE ON METHODOLOGY

I am often asked about the methodology used in collecting information for *Food for Thought*. Essentially, there were three sources of information.

For many years I visited and lived with different groups of people eating different foods and observed their behavior. These groups ranged from the American Indians of the south and southwestern United States to the Indians of the Punjab and south India. During this period I visited clinics, centers and experts in North America and Europe, observing and discussing how diet is used (and abused) in health care. These investigations brought me to psychiatric clinics, longevity centers and natural-food communities in America and to health retreats, allergy clinics and vegetarian societies in Britain. All of these experiences provide a fascinating source of information.

However, they are fraught with two fundamental methodological problems: One is the problem of selective perception, the other is the relationship of correlation and causality. Stated simply, selective perception implies that the observer often *un-consciously* sees those observations that support his beliefs and hypotheses, failing to see those that do not. This is a problem of the ethological approach to research in which the observer does not control the variables of the experimental situation but simply notes what he observes happening around him. The idea that correlation doesn't imply causality means that one can't determine or define the causal factors of any two stimuli or events that occur together. For example, in seeing a group of people eating certain foods and behaving in a certain way, one can't determine if their behavior is influenced by their diet or if their diet is a function of their behavior. These factors must be considered.

A second source of observation for *Food for Thought* was based on my own eating experience and my personal experimentation with food. For the past fifteen years my wife, Dr. Jo Anne Miller, and I have experienced many "diets"—the high-protein, low-protein, vegetarian and macrobiotic diets, the extreme meat and sugar diet of America...and fasting. During this period I noticed some substantial changes in my health and behavior. For example, my weight which fifteen years ago was a muscular 200 pounds dropped to 120 pounds (in 1972) before levelling off at my present 165 pounds. These changes were accompanied by changes in energy level, attitudes, sensitivity, and motivation. Of course, there are large individual differences in reaction to different foods, and one must be cautious not to overgeneralize from one's own experience. Whenever possible, I have attempted to discuss and corroborate my findings with others who have experimented with and experienced different diets. Though self-report and personal experimentation do not provide as reliable and objective a source of data as "scientific" experimentation, they do provide a real source of information. People seem to enjoy talking about food, and I have been impressed with the openness with which people throughout the world have dicussed their dietary experiences with me.

In my clinical practice I counsel people about improving the quality of life. One of the factors that I feel is basic to their sense of well-being is what and how they eat. Over the years I have advised many people to change their diets in specific ways and have observed the results. This information is also an important part of *Food for Thought*.

The third source of information for this book comes from the scientific investigation of the relationship of food and behavior. "Scientific" in this sense means *controlled* experimentation with food. Perhaps the two most significant observations that can be made about this relationship are that (1) surprisingly little research has been done, and (2) what has been done suggests that the food we eat has a marked effect on how we think, feel and act.

For ethical, social, nutritional and pleasurable reasons, it seems that people do not volunteer and are rarely used as subjects in nutritional experiments. Over 90 percent of the nutritional research is carried out with small mammals (rats and Guinea pigs) as subjects. Quite naturally, it is extremely difficult to generalize and define from these animal studies the subtle differences in human behavior that occur as a function of diet.

I have tried on several occasions to conduct controlled research on food using members of the general public as subjects. (I have also participated in such research as a subject.) My experience has been that people will rarely submit themselves to any investigation controlling their diet for any length of time. In one study I carried out at Schiller College in London, England, twenty-four student volunteers were divided into two groups and asked to eat either cooked or raw food *exclusively* for three days. After a three-day baseline the conditions were reversed. (All subjects recorded their behavior on three dimensions, three times daily for twelve days.) In a frank and open discussion of the experiment after the data were collected, subjects were told that the experimenter was not seeking to support his hypotheses but to find out what had happened. It was explained that any failure to eat according to the rules of the experiment wasn't "bad," and was in fact significant information. So informed, twenty-two of twenty-four subjects reported that they had *not* followed the experimental procedure. While no doubt there has been some controlled human research on food and behavior (e.g. the Keyes study of conscientious objectors), lack of cooperation and inability to regulate food intake make this research difficult. Often groups who willingly volunteer and participate in such research have a certain dietary point of view, and they want to demonstrate that their dietary principles or philosophy of life is "right." As such, they present something of a biased sample for food and behavior research.

What findings do exist, from both human and animal studies, suggest that food and nutrition have a marked effect on health and behavior. Many of these findings are reported in *Food for Thought*. They, along with information on traditional dietary patterns and my personal and clinical experience, form the substance of this book.

I would be pleased if *Food for Thought* stimulates others to eat sensibly and to conduct research on food and behavior. Both are important and are to be encouraged.

FOOD FOR THOUGHT

Man is literally made from the dust of the earth. For this reason, his psychological and mental activities are profoundly influenced by the geological constitution of the country where he lives, by the nature of the animals and plants on which he feeds.

Alexis Carrel, *Man, The Unknown*[1]

FOOD = ENERGY = BEHAVIOR

Man, our food, and our behavior are all forms of the same energy. The nature of the energy we take in as food shapes our nature, and influences the energy we express as behavior.

Our daily diet is a basic factor enabling us to maximize our potential, performance, and pleasure, or limiting both our sanity and satisfaction.

Introduction

Chapter **1**

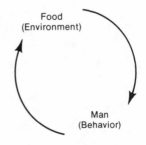

Food
(Environment)

Man
(Behavior)

Of course, many factors influence our behavior. Four major determinants are:

1. **Our constitution**—what we inherit from our parents. This acquisition predisposes us to act in certain ways. It does not necessarily follow that we develop our potentialities or express our limitations or that we are merely what we are given.
2. **Our conditioning**—what we have learned in life. Our education, training, and experience of life have a marked effect on how we behave. While our earliest learning experiences are most significant, we are capable of learning, growing, and changing throughout life.
3. **Our external environment**—what's happening out there What is the situation or the demands confronting us? What has to be done and what we have available to do it with will also determine our behavior.
4. **Our internal environment**—what's happening inside us: the state of our internal being, the functioning of our organs, the quality of our blood. *Our nervous system works by the transmission of electro-chemical impulses. If our biochemistry is disordered, then our behavior is also disordered.*

Our constitution, conditioning, and external environment all affect our biochemistry, however, and there is nothing more basic to it and how we behave than the food we eat. Moreover, of the factors listed above, there is none over which we have greater control than our diet.

FOOD AND BRAIN FUNCTION

Our brains are highly complex, multifunctional organs, comprised of billions of cells which intercommunicate or "run" on electro-chemical impulses. A healthy or natural biochemistry produces reliable, integrated brain function, sanity and satisfaction. In contrast, an unhealthy biochemistry disrupts the function of the nervous system and behavior.

The food we eat affects and determines our biochemical make-up. When our diet is unbalanced, uncentered, and unnatural, our brain function is disrupted. The ensuing disorder is both mental and physical and may be expressed as: actions divorced from thoughts; ideas out of harmony with instinctive patterns and bio-logical rhythms; limited perspectives; and limited self-control. The end result is the same: a reduction of performance and pleasure, feelings of depression, anxiety, and fear (neurosis) and sometimes a sense of being disoriented or lost (psychosis).

THE BASICS OF SANE EATING

Section **I**

*Steak and eggs are contractive; fruits, candy and beer
are expansive; and bread is in the middle.*

The basis of *Food for Thought* is *understanding* food and its effects
and what to eat to be sane and satisfied. To appreciate food in a
total and *practical* way we present it on a single dimension. The
poles of this dimension we call *expansion* and *contraction*. All food
can be divided into three groups, each with its own place on this
scale.

1. Animal foods (meat, fish, eggs and dairy) are on the contractive end of the dimension.
2. Plant foods (grains, vegetables and fruits) are in the center.
3. Plant derivatives (sugar, spices, alcohol and drugs) are on
   the expansive end.

Food:
A Total View

Chapter **2**

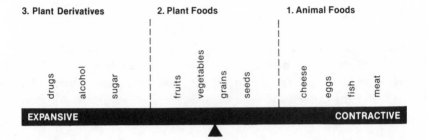

Animal Foods. Animal foods are contractive simply because most of the animals we eat are concentrated vegetable energy. That is, animals eat and grow on a diet of grasses and grains—which becomes their flesh. It has been estimated that between five and ten pounds of vegetable protein produce one pound of animal protein.* In this sense animals are more concentrated or contractive than plants.

While all animal foods are contractive, some are more contractive than others. Red meat is the most contractive, more than fowl (and eggs), fish and dairy food. Of the latter, cheese and butter are more concentrated or contractive than milk. There may be ten pounds of milk in one pound of butter or cheese.

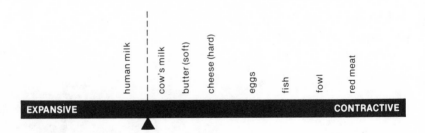

---

*If a family of four were to eat just grain and vegetables for a year, they would require less than an acre of land to grow all their food. If that same family were to eat just beef more than ten times the acreage would be required to support the cattle, and thus their appetite.

Plant Foods. Plant foods occupy the center of the dimension and form the main part of the human diet. They range from seeds (such as grains, nuts and beans) on the contractive side to grapes, melons, and tropical fruits on the expansive end. Vegetables are in between.

Within the plant foods, the smaller, harder, more compact ones, and those growing more slowly or below ground, are more contractive. The larger, leafier, juicier plants growing quickly or above ground are more expansive.

Fruits are more expansive than vegetables. When we eat fruits, we eat or drink the sweeter, juicier, more expansive parts of the plant. Smaller, denser fruits, such as berries, cherries and apples, are more contractive than a bunch of grapes or a melon.

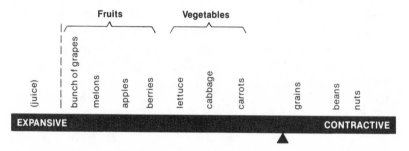

Most natural foods fall into these two groups. However, there is a third group which I will call plant derivatives. This group belongs at the expansive end of the dimension.

Plant Derivatives. Plant derivatives are extracts, concentrates and distillates of various parts of the plant. Included in this group are sugar, syrups, tea, coffee, wine, beer, spirits, marijuana and other drugs. I refer to them as expansive for two reasons:

1. They are usually made from the most expansive part of the plant—its fruit, juices, blossoms or leaves.
2. These substances have a marked effect on the nervous system and an expansive effect on behavior.

L.S.D. | marijuana "drugs" | distilled spirits (liquor) | wine, beer | chemical sweeteners | sugar | coffee | syrup | fruit juices

EXPANSIVE — CONTRACTIVE

These derivatives are *not* whole foods. For example: *Fruit juices* are the most expansive (liquid, sweet) part of the plant. Most commercial fruit juices are pressed, boiled and filtered. *Syrups* are made by extracting and boiling down the juice from fruits (and vegetables). By further processing syrups, one gets *sugar*. White sugar is further refined. *Alcoholic drinks* (wine, beer, spirits) are produced by the fermentation, brewing, and distillation of more centered foods (fruits, vegetables, and grains). *Coffee and tea* are derived by processing and leaching beans and leaves.

The table that follows will help you to classify foods according to their expansive or contractive properties.

	EXPANSIVE	CONTRACTIVE
Size	larger	smaller
Location	above ground	below ground
Growth Rate	fast	slow
Texture	soft	hard
Moisture	liquid, juicy	solid, dry
Taste	sweet, sour	salty, bitter
Nature	vegetable	animal
Climate	moderate, warm	extreme cold (desert)
Preparation	less cooking (raw)	more cooking
Movement	outwards	inwards
Chemical	potassium	sodium*

*Healthy neurological transmission is maintained by the appropriate potassium/sodium balance. Neurological transmission is intimately related to the food we eat.

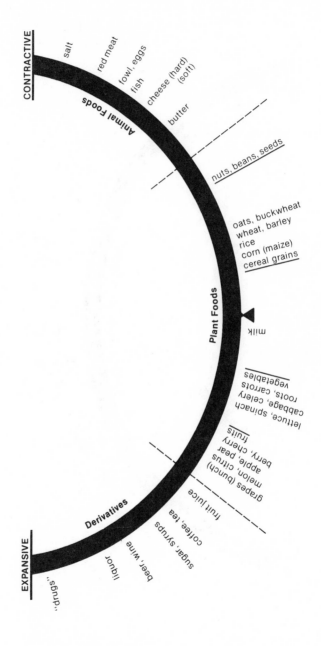

CONTRACTIVE

salt
red meat
fowl, eggs
fish
cheese (hard)
(soft)
butter

Animal Foods

nuts, beans, seeds

oats, buckwheat
wheat, barley
rice
corn (maize)
cereal grains

Plant Foods

milk

vegetables
roots, carrots
cabbage, celery
lettuce, spinach

fruits
berry, cherry
apple, pear
melon, citrus
grapes (bunch)

fruit juice

coffee, tea
sugar, syrups

Derivatives

beer, wine
liquor
"drugs"

EXPANSIVE

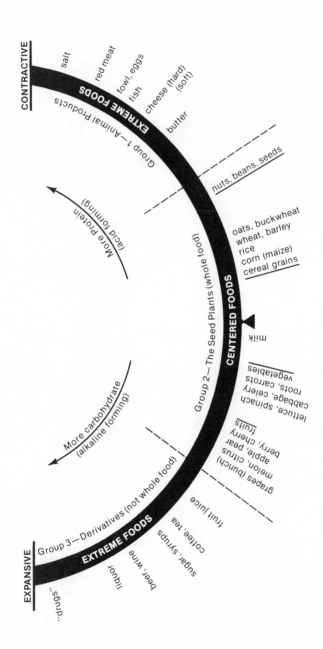

CONTRACTIVE

salt
red meat
fowl, eggs
fish
cheese (hard)
(soft)
butter

EXTREME FOODS

Group 1—Animal Products

nuts, beans, seeds

More protein
(acid forming)

Group 2— The Seed Plants (whole food)

CENTERED FOODS

oats, buckwheat
wheat, barley
rice
corn (maize)
cereal grains

milk

lettuce, spinach
cabbage, celery
roots, carrots
vegetables

berry, cherry
apple, pear
melon, citrus
grapes (bunch)
fruits

More carbohydrate
(alkaline forming)

fruit juice

Group 3—Derivatives (not whole food)

EXTREME FOODS

coffee, tea
sugar, syrups
beer, wine
liquor
"drugs"

EXPANSIVE

If all this seems a bit confusing or just too much, then re-member:

Steak and eggs are contractive; fruits, candy and beer are expansive; and bread is in the middle.

Nutritionists usually classify food in terms of its acidity-alkalinity, its vitamin, mineral, protein, calorie or carbohydrate content. These are all determined by chemical analysis of the food in the laboratory. In these terms, acidity-alkalinity and protein: carbohydrate ratio are consistent with our classification of the food in groups 1 and 2 (whole foods) as expansive and contractive.*

The advantage of using terms like expansive and contractive rather than the nutritionist's terms mentioned above is that expansion and contraction are *universal* concepts. That is:

- They classify foods on the basis of many factors (not simply vitamin, or mineral, or protein content).
- They can be easily understood.
- They can be applied meaningfully not just to food, but to all natural phenomena, including behavior. As you shall see, expansive food ⟶ expansive behavior, contractive food ⟶ contractive behavior.

---

*Protein:carbohydrate ratio is simply the amount of protein relative to the amount of carbohydrate in any food. This index can be calculated from the data provided in most food composition tables.[1] Generally, contractive foods have a high protein:carbohydrate ratio, while expansive foods have a low protein:carbohydrate ratio. Generally, acid-forming foods are contractive while alkaline-forming foods are expansive.

Biologists have observed that all living things are motivated by a need for homeostasis, the continuous balancing of life systems. Some psychologists have described life as a balancing of man's creative (eros) and destructive (thanatos) instincts. Balance in all things including diet may be seen as an interplay between the forces of expansion and contraction.

Throughout life, people select their food (often unconsciously) to satisfy their tastes and hungers, and to meet the demands of their environment, constitution and life style. Of course, a newborn infant cannot select its food. It must be content with the perfectly balanced food that has evolved to provide its nourishment—(mother's) milk.

Human milk is the one food that experts universally agree to be appropriate to our species. In terms of our classification it is

How to
Balance a Diet

Chapter **3**

relatively balanced, for it is neither expansive nor contractive. Human milk has a protein:carbohydrate ratio of between 1:6–1:8. (Cow's milk and goat's milk are more contractive and have a protein:carbohydrate ratio of between 1:1–1:2.)

As we get older and can voluntarily select food for ourselves, our diets become extremely varied. However, throughout our lives the same dietary balance between expansion and contraction —or a protein:carbohydrate ratio of about 1:7—is generally maintained.

EXPANSIVE	"drugs"	alcohol	sugar	fruits	vegetables	human milk	grains	cow's milk	beans, nuts	cheese	eggs	fish	meat	CONTRACTIVE
(Protein: Carbohydrate Ratio)			0:99	1:2	1:9	1:7		1:2		10:1	15:1		25:0	

HOW TO BALANCE YOUR DIET

There are many ways of making balance. Some are easier than others. If you eat lots of meat, which is extremely contractive (and has a protein:carbohydrate ratio of 25:0), you will be attracted to extremely expansive foods such as sweets and sugar (which are high in carbohydrate but have no protein—p:c = 0:99) to make balance. That is to say, *extreme expansion balances extreme contraction, or sweet balances meat. This is the law of opposites.*

Balancing in the extremes is possible. It is the way that most people eat in America and Europe today. However, since it consumes more energy than balancing near the center, it is wasteful, stressful, and tiring.

You have probably had at one point in your life some experience on a see-saw and some understanding of balancing it. It is simpler to balance two objects near the center (A in illustration below) than the same two objects on the extremes (B in illustration below). A slight variation in the former will have a much less disruptive effect than a slight variation in the latter. The same principles apply to diet. It is much easier *and less stressful* to balance foods more central on the continuum, for example, grains and vegetables, than it is to balance foods in the extremes, for example, sugar and meat.

A

B

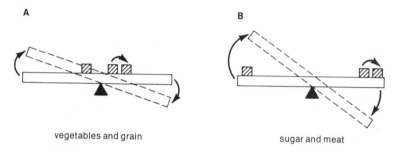

vegetables and grain

sugar and meat

A balanced diet is a part of a balanced lifestyle; an unbalanced diet correlates with disordered behavior. *The manner in which people select their foods and make balance is a basic factor determining their behavior.*

As a schoolboy, I was taught that a balanced diet was one with plenty of red meat, eggs, whole milk, cheese, and fresh green vegetables and some fruit. As you can see, this is unbalancing. In

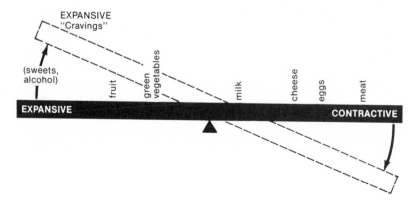

terms of our classification, it appears to be weighted on the contractive end of the scale. It is a diet that leads to cravings for expansive foods like sugar, sweets, alcohol, and even drugs. In my case, it nurtured a fabulous sweet tooth. It is also a diet that affects behavior in certain definite ways.

God created man in His own image, in the image of God created He him: male and female created He them. And God blessed them: and God said unto them: "Be fruitful, and multiply, and replenish the earth, and subdue it: and have dominion over the fish of the sea, and over the fowl of the air and over every living thing that moveth upon the earth."

And God said: "Behold I have given you every herb bearing seed, which is upon the face of all the earth, and every tree, in which is the fruit of a tree yielding seed; to you it shall be for food...."

Genesis 1:27-29[1]

Since the time of creation, much has been said about what we should and shouldn't eat. Cross-cultural study makes it clear

Man's Principal Food

Chapter **4**

that no one food is critical. People survive and even thrive eating all kinds of different plants and animals.

The first Biblical prescription of the appropriate food for man suggests it is "every herb yielding seed...and the fruit of a tree yielding seed" (Genesis 1:29). So described, man's foods are the seed-bearing plants. This includes the full range of plant foods (group 2) from fruits and vegetables (expansive) to grains, beans, nuts, and seeds (contractive). Of this group, grains are the most complete. In grains, the fruit and the seed are one.

For the past 10,000 years, man has been eating cereal grain as his principal food. Grains are the seeds of domesticated grasses and include: rice, wheat, oats, rye, barley, maize (corn), millet, and buckwheat.*

> *In biological terms, man is a grass-seed eater and the fortunes of his civilization are preconditioned by the skill with which he has been able to breed and adapt his grains to various soils and climatic conditions.* [2]

Wheat was the principal grain for most of Europe, the Middle East and later North America; corn was prevalent throughout the Americas and parts of Africa; millet in parts of Asia, Africa and Europe; rye in Northern Europe; and rice in the Far East. There have been some regional variations (e.g., oats for the Celts, buckwheat for the Russians, and corn for the Roumanians). However, there has been little change in this pattern until recent times.

Grains are used in various forms. Wheat, oats, rye and maize are usually ground into flour or meal for some kind of bread or porridge. Buckwheat is eaten as groats (kasha) or made into flour for noodles (soba). Barley is ground in bread or gruel and malted in beer. Millet and rice are most usually eaten in grain form.

Today, grain remains the principal food for over three-quarters of mankind. [3]

---

*Buckwheat is not actually a cereal grain.

OUR DAILY BREAD

Grain is almost as basic to the human adult as mother's milk is to the infant. Both are relatively balanced foods, with a protein: carbohydrate ratio of about 1:7.

Europeans describe bread as the staff of life, an idea they share with the Americans who refer to the family provider as the "breadwinner" and money as "bread" or "dough."

English-speaking people call their thrice-daily "meals," which simply means ground grain. The Japanese similarly refer to their meals as *gohan,* which means rice, their principal food.

Jewish law defines a meal and requires the appropriate prayers at any feeding at which grain (bread) is eaten.

The Christian Lord's Prayer begin its supplications with "Give us this day our daily bread." Christ and David before Him came from the line of Bethlehem—a lineage whose Hebrew name literally means house (*beth*) of bread (*lechem*).

FOOD AND BEHAVIOR

For thousands of years, our species has eaten grain along with a variety of secondary foods...meats, fish, dairy, nuts, fruits and vegetables. With this diet, food and behavior interrelated in a predictable fashion.

As a general rule, those who lived where it was colder and the climate was more extreme, hence contracting, ate more contractive foods (such as meat and fish) with their grain and behaved in a more contractive manner. Contrastingly, those who lived where and when it was warmer and more moderate ate more expansive foods (like fruits and vegetables) with their daily meal and behaved in a more expansive manner. To summarize this relationship:

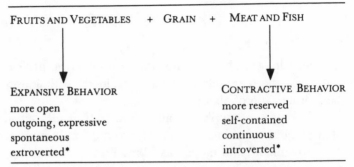

FRUITS AND VEGETABLES   +   GRAIN   +   MEAT AND FISH

EXPANSIVE BEHAVIOR   CONTRACTIVE BEHAVIOR
more open   more reserved
outgoing, expressive   self-contained
spontaneous   continuous
extroverted*   introverted*

*That's not to say that extroversion and introversion correlate perfectly with an expansive or contractive diet but rather that expansive foods increase extroversion and a contractive diet increases introverted behavior.

In times of plenty, the tendency has been to omit grain and other central foods from the diet. Refined and adulterated cereal grains have been relegated to the role of secondary fillers. In their place, people are eating increasing amounts of extreme (e.g. meat ◀——▶ sugar, alcohol) and unnatural (chemically processed, instant) foods.

The simple relationship of food and behavior just described is being obscured by new dietary habits and extreme and unnatural behavior patterns.

Understanding the principles, you are free to choose.
Practicing the principles, you are free to enjoy.

"WHAT SHOULD I EAT?"

I generally advise people to eat a centered, balanced diet of natural foods.

Within that broad prescription, it is for *you* to decide what to eat for yourself.

In the past, choices were governed by availability and tradition. In the old days, people were often content if they simply had enough of whatever was available. Today the marketplace is overflowing with a wide variety of foods... some familiar, some novel, some from near and some from faraway, some wholesome, some not. We are now free to pick and choose our food according to our needs and tastes. Indeed, we *must* now exercise a conscious choice in order to maintain our well-being.

The
Ten Principles
of Sane Eating

Chapter **5**

But many people select their foods unconsciously. Often they are unaware of how food affects their mental health and happiness. While many of the foods available to us have changed, the same principles and consequences of eating exist today as they have throughout the ages.

THE TEN PRINCIPLES
OF SANE EATING

In my research, travels, and practice, I have experienced ten principles of sane and healthy eating. They are shown in the following table.

1. Expansive food ⟶	expansive behavior
2. Contractive food ⟶	contractive behavior
3. Expansive food ⟷	contractive food*
4. Extreme food ⟶	extreme behavior
5. A centered diet ⟶	a centered (balanced) disposition
6. Natural food ⟶	natural behavior
7. Dis-integrated food ⟶	dis-integrated behavior
8. Alien food ⟶	alienation
9. Fatty food ⟶	blocks energy flow, reduces sensitivity, and vitality
10. Overeating ⟶	reduces sensitivity, vitality, and attractiveness

*The law of opposites.

Though each of us is unique, and though our diets may differ somewhat, the same ten principles apply to us all. Understanding and *using* these principles will increase your health and happiness.

In the chapters that follow I will discuss these principles, the relationship of present-day diets to present-day behavior, and what and how to eat to be sane, satisfied, and attractive.

"Making balance" in life comes from an awareness of the extremes and a familiarity with the center. Making balance with food follows an appreciation of which foods are extreme, what are their consequences, and how best they combine with the more centered principal foods.

MAKING BALANCE

Section **II**

A centered diet ———▶ a centered disposition.

I enjoy talking to people about food. It is one subject about which everyone has some experience and usually something to say.

I discussed healthy eating with a food-conscious physician and his wife from the American Midwest. The doctor listed the properties of a healthy diet as follows: one with a broad selection of fresh foods, vegetables, salads and fruits; some animal food including fish, eggs, lean meat; but no milk, no processed foods, no white bread and no sugar.

I agreed with his point of view but noted there was one major omission. He had not included any whole grain in his "perfect" diet. He smiled and replied, "But that's an Oriental custom. If I were to adopt an Oriental diet, my body would probably rebel, just as an Oriental's would if he started eating my food." When I

Centering

Chapter **6**

asked the doctor and his wife where their ancestors came from, he said his were from England and Wales and hers were from Germany and Holland. I reminded them that just a few generations ago their ancestors ate wheat, oats and rye as their *main* food and the notion of grains as a principal food was by no means exclusively Oriental. Until recently, it was an almost universal eating pattern, but one that people are rapidly forgetting.

When your principal foods are selected from the *middle* of the food dimension, then your diet is *centered*.

The absence of a centered principal food can have an un-centering or unbalancing effect on behavior. This uncenteredness may be reflected in posture, emotional stability, and one's overall perspective.

POSTURE

Three postures illustrate the difference between centered and uncentered individuals.

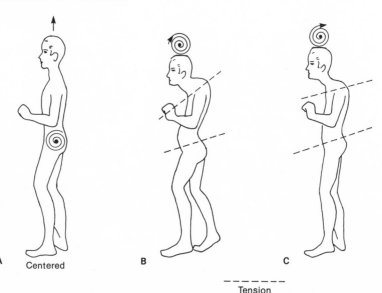

A   Centered   B   C

– – – – – – –
Tension

The A posture represents the centered person who can't easily be upset. The gravitational center is in the mid-body ⊚ allowing for greater balance and control; the head is upright with the sense organs well presented and the organism poised to respond with flexibility, control and grace in any direction.

B and C are two extreme uncentered postures. Both represent bodies that are somewhat disconnected and easily unbalanced. In terms of diet, both correlate with extreme eating habits. (Posture B is more characteristic of people who have been habitually eating lots of meat and other contractive foods, while posture C is more characteristic of a history of lots of sweets, sugar and expansive drugs.)

Your posture is just one indication of your psychophysical orientation but, like diet, it correlates directly with your personality. If your posture is centered and balanced, then you are more inclined to be centered and balanced; that is, you are more apt to be emotionally stable and less susceptible to outside or extraneous influences.[1]

One middle-aged housewife I counseled appeared to evaluate herself by looking in the mirror and listening to the compliments that others paid her. She was overweight, round-shouldered and depressed. "I was always quite attractive," she cried, "but recently I began to look old and fat and I wanted to die."

When I asked her what she ate she explained that she knew a lot about diet. For years she had been "dieting" and following what she thought was sound nutritional advice. She rarely ate any carbohydrates. Rather, she fed on the extremes: high protein foods (such as meat, eggs and cheese), salads, plenty of fruit juices, artificial diet drinks and food supplements.

Her self-perception, like her diet, was peripheral and uncentered. She was concerned with tastes, appearances and impressions and was herself quite impressionable, easily disappointed and depressed.

As a part of counseling, I explained that her diet was influencing her behavior and appearance. I advised that in order to feel and look younger, and to be more *centered, stable* and *balanced,* at least a third of her diet should consist of whole grains, and that she should continue avoiding all *refined* carbohydrates (e.g., sugar, white flour, and any foods containing these substances).

One couple sought advice because they were extremely concerned about their teenage son, whom they had labelled a slow learner. He appeared to me intelligent and sensitive, yet his parents chose to perceive him as too short and too passive. It might be said that the parents were not getting on well and projected some of their frustrations onto "things" other than themselves. They had heard that I knew something about food and psychology and asked if I could recommend a diet to accelerate their son's development. They were very interested in food, but followed an un-centered high-protein diet.

I reminded the parents that good things didn't always come in large packages and suggested a centered, wholesome diet for their son similar to that described in the chapter on recommendations. They greeted my response with some distress. Another expert had advised hormone injections along with a high-protein diet which included large quantities of animal food, especially whole milk. "Everyone says something different," they protested. "How do we decide what to do?"

I remarked that they were apt to find that there were as many opinions as there were experts. I advised them that a whole-grain based diet with fewer extreme, dairy, and processed foods would benefit them as well as their son. Over time, it would help them to become more centered and perhaps better able to decide which advice to follow in the future.

In the 1950s, sociologists in America reported a shift from the inner-directed to the outer-directed personality. They observed that people had become less self-determining, self-evaluating and centered in themselves (inner-directed), and had come to define themselves, their goals and successes more in terms of others (outer-directed).[2] Along with these changes, they described a shift in eating habits to being less centered and more taste (tongue) oriented. These changes correlate with changes in posture and with the great social and environmental changes of the post-war period. No change, however, was more basic and more drastic than that of diet (illustrated below[3]).

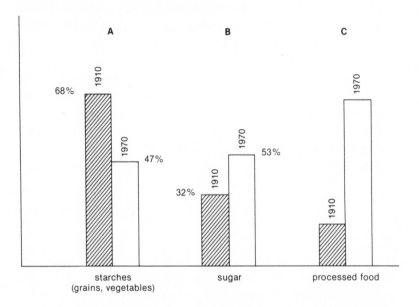

Since the period just prior to the First World War, the consumption of whole grains has decreased almost 50 percent and the increase in uncentered diets with high proportions of refined, extreme and synthetic foods has been astronomical.

Until recently there had been no systematic psychological experiments correlating food with posture and self-perception. Only in the past few years have studies begun to define the lack of self-awareness and centeredness of today's educated young people.

In one such study carried out at a New York university, a group of male college students were hooked up to electrical apparatus and told it would measure their heart rate. Once wired, the subjects were asked to select from a stack of pictures of semi-nude females those they found to be most attractive. While the pictures (slides) of the female were being presented to them, each subject could hear amplifications of his heartbeat sound over a loud speaker system.

The results showed clearly and significantly that the subjects reported the pictures accompanied by the faster heartbeat sounds to be more attractive than those that were accompanied by slower heartbeat sounds. It appears that attraction and a racing heart go together, but then that's no surprise.

It turns out, however, that the heartbeat sounds were in fact bogus, or fake. There were contrived noises—manipulations by the experimenters that had nothing whatsoever to do with the subjects' true cardiac responses. The conclusion is that these young men cued the scientific feedback rather than themselves to determine their feelings.[4]

PERSPECTIVES

Many people I speak with tell me that they are not eating as they should. Generally, food is low in their list of priorities. If they're rushed, busy, socially pressed, depressed, inconvenienced or just wanting to let go, it's often their diet that suffers. They are either unaware or ignore the fact that what they eat reflects and determines how they think, feel and act.

A centered diet with whole grains as a principal food can provide some perspective to lifestyle. If location, vocation or domestic situation make a grain based diet impossible or impractical, it is often an indication that lifestyle is extreme and in need of some centering.

I met with a group of physiotherapists who were interested in learning how food affects posture with a view to improving their health and practice. I spoke of grain as being man's principal food and described a diet of whole grains and vegetables with smaller quantities of fruit, beans and animal food. Most of the therapists seemed interested and agreeable to what had been said. However, one woman remarked, "It sounds great, but it isn't practical. I work from nine to six, six days a week, and I just don't have the time to cook."

I agreed that it does require some time to prepare wholesome food, but not as much as she might think. I have known a good many active people who take time to eat right. Besides, I told her, some time and order in the kitchen can improve the quality of life.

A London-based artist I have been friendly with for many years is moody and unstable. He lives and works in frantic bursts of energy. His domestic life is chaotic, his romantic affairs often violent and his home a menagerie of assorted animals.

Over the years, he has been a frequent dinner guest. He reliably extols the virtue of home cooked, centered food, but explains that he hasn't the time to shop and cook these meals for himself. He also expressed some concern that this food might not be able to support the passionate quality of his life.

Such problems as lack of time or space, being too busy, too alone, or too passionate to eat in a centered and orderly fashion often highlight disorder or imbalance in lifestyle.

A centered principal food diet need not be restrictive or narrow. Most traditional diets have consisted of grain as the principal food with smaller quantities of a variety of secondary foods. It has been said of the Chinese that their diet was rice and beans, rice and fish, rice and vegetables, rice and meat, rice and fruit, rice and wine, and rice and rice.

A centered principal food, combined with lesser quantities of more expansive and contractive foods, enables you to be open to a broad range of stimulation and at the same time provides stability and helps you to maintain your perspective.

Many people advocate food reform and adopt new eating habits. Some become vegetarians, some eat meat, some cook their foods, some eat them raw, some take vitamins, some don't, some are stable and some are not. Change, of course, does not mean that the new eating habits nurture physical and mental health. For example, some people adopt a broad spectrum vegetarian diet *without any central food*. They eat plenty of fruits, salads, raw foods, honey and yoghurt and gallons of fruit juice. Often their attraction to these expansive foods results from a history of eating very contractive foods (meat, eggs and salt) and living in contracting circumstances (cities, crowding, and stress) for many years. While this pattern is understandable, it regularly leads to a lack of direction, emotional liability (emotional ups and downs) and confusion.

I spoke to a food reform group in England. Many of the members were raw eaters who had no centered principal food in their diet.* They were friendly and pleasant to be with. However, their meeting was characterized by disorganization, an excess of opinions and chatter and a lack of direction and order. Later, about fifty people volunteered to complete a personality inventory that I was handing out which demanded yes or no answers to about one hundred questions. Many respondents either didn't want to, or couldn't, confine their answers to the simple yes or no that was required. Rather, they frequently responded to both items, omitted questions, and some wrote long emotionally charged comments throughout the questionnaire. It was an interesting exercise, but not the one called for on this occasion.

Vegetarianism can, of course, be practiced with a centered principal food. Indeed, many people have reported that a grain-based vegetarian oriented diet has helped them to be more centered and stable.

EAT SIMPLY

You can also reduce confusion by eating simply. A balanced diet does not mean eating a bit of everything at one meal. Eating simply

---

*Raw eating is discussed in Chapter 19.

implies eating foods that combine well together and not eating too much or too many foods at any one time.

Different foods are processed by different parts of the digestive system at different rates of speed. Hence, it is advisable to eat foods that are digestively compatible, or that "combine" well together.[5] In general, grains combine well with vegetables, but poorly with fruits, sweets (sugar, honey, jams, etc.) and fats (oil, butter, peanut butter, etc.), as illustrated on page 36.

Vegetables (especially leafy, green vegetables) combine well with grains and beans, animal foods, and fatty foods. However, starchy vegetables (like potato) and cereal grains do not combine well together.

Fruits are best eaten by themselves. They do not combine well with other foods. If you are mixing fruit and other foods, it's advisable to eat the fruit first, wait a while, then eat the other food.

Sugar interferes with the digestion of most foods. Poor combinations include sugar in recipes and prepared foods, and sweet dessert immediately after a meal.

Select your food intelligently, and limit the number of different foods you eat at any one time. Eat simply.

There is a tale of four travellers sitting in a small caravanserai eating the food they had brought for their journey. "I always eat almond paste and coriander seed cakes with sugar plums," said the rich merchant. "I eat honey mixed with oats and dried mulberries," said the soldier. "I eat dried curds and pistachio nuts with apricot puree," said the scholar.

Having said their pieces, they all turned to the sufi wise man Nasrudin. "I never eat anything but wheat, mixed with wheat and then carefully baked," said the sufi, taking out a piece of bread.

It has been said, "If you are entertaining a sufi, remember dry bread is enough."[6] This expression says something of bread and of the man. It does not imply that bread should be man's sole food, but rather that (wholemeal) bread is sufficient to sustain life and health. Of the sufi, it reflects his health and perspective, for he can be content with what is sufficient.

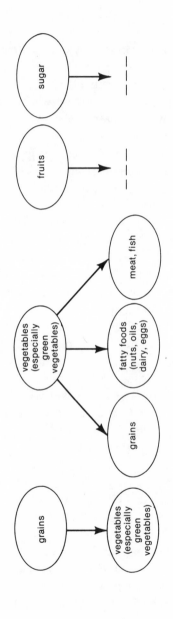

CENTERING YOUR DIET

In olden days, most people living in temperate regions ate a diet of between 50–75 percent grain along with 10–20 percent animal food. They spent most of their time outdoors and were physically very active. Whole grains stimulate and require physical exercise.

Today, people live a more sedentary and centrally heated existence, and they exercise less. Generally, I advise about 30–35 percent whole grains. The specific amount appropriate to any one person varies according to that person's age, constitution, activity pattern, vocation, location, and the time of year. Whatever the quantity or the means of preparation, the grains should be 100 percent whole. Refined food is a cause of mental and physical disorder.

Today's diets are uncentered and extreme. Each year, the average American consumes 240 pounds of meat, 120 pounds of sugar and less than 10 pounds of whole grain.

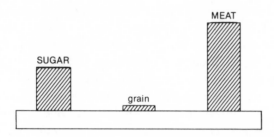

Extremes

Chapter **7**

Extreme food leads to extreme behavior. If your diet is un-centered and extreme, then you are more inclined to be subject to extreme desires, extreme thoughts and extreme actions.

Almost every one of us has the ability to control our behavior. However, eating an extreme diet makes self-control more difficult and, in the process, increases tension, frustration, stress and disease.

There is a man known to many Londoners who parades around the downtown shopping area with a signboard that reads "Less protein, less passion." He advocates that high-protein foods such as meat, fish, eggs, cheese, nuts and beans create excessive passion which he believes is the cause of much of today's social unrest. He is particularly concerned with the unhappiness engendered through insatiable sexual appetites and insensitive sexual expression. While I understand his point of view, I feel his sales pitch is somewhat misdirected. I once suggested to him that his placard might be more effective if it read "Less protein, greater sensitivity and pleasure."

His thesis is not a new one. Over 3,000 years ago, Pythagoras advocated a diet of low protein foods—grains, fruits, herbs and *no no* meat, fish, eggs or beans—as a means to greater sensitivity and social and sexual equality.[1]

Sexual behavior is affected by the extreme meat and sugar diet of the modern adult. Meat intensifies sexual urges and reduces sensitivity while sugar increases fantasy and reduces vitality.* The end result is strong urges and strange ideas about sex. This diet nurtures widespread sexual preoccupations, pornography and disintegrated, insensitive sexual relations. There are many people who experience anxiety and unhappiness as a result of not being able to satisfy disproportional sexual desires or ideals stimulated by an extreme diet. (Food and sexual behavior are discussed in Chapter 16.)

Extreme foods also contribute to unnecessary violence. As people eat more and more extreme foods, behavior has become

---

*In moderate amounts, meat may stimulate sexual desire; in large quantities, it appears to have the effect of reducing sexual drive.

more destructive and intense. For example, childbeating has been increasing in frequency and, according to one expert, the Los Angeles coroner, child killings have become more violent and brutal.[2]

Anyone who has been caught up in an excited mob knows the extreme uncontrollable quality of its energy. I have been in the midst of groups of agitated young people in Europe, Asia, North Africa and North America. For many, it has appeared that the cause of the mob's gathering, be it a political demonstration or a rock festival, was of secondary significance. What seemed most important was the chance to release tension and excessive energy. In this century, the more non-violent demonstrations have had their birth and greatest success amongst people eating diets low in protein.

Of course diet is not the sole cause of violence, nor is it a sufficient condition. Self-control is almost always possible. However, *an extreme diet makes self-control more difficult and less likely.* When it interacts with dissatisfying socio-economic conditions, an extreme diet often produces behavior characterized by uncontrollable outbursts of energy.

Law and enforcement agencies are sometimes necessary to control behavior. Such action is, however, peripheral, imposing restraint from the outside (from inner-directed to outer-directed). An alternative approach is to increase internal control. One way this can be accomplished is by moving diet away from the extremes back to a more central space in which people are more inclined to behave in a sane, sensitive and self-controlled manner.

At the turn of the century, psychiatrists, led by Freud, described how personalities and problems were created by the way a person expressed, redirected, and held back varying intensities of life energy (libido). They said the prime cause of mental disorder was the inability to satisfy libidinal drives within society. No mention was made of how food affected life energy at that time.

Now it is clear that extreme diets unnecessarily intensify the need (tension) to express or to inhibit energy. Eating meat and sugar in the quantities that most Americans do leads to marked increases in physical hypertension or high blood pressure and heart disease. These disorders affect one in every three Americans. Physical hypertension correlates with psychological hypertension. That is, high blood pressure correlates with feelings of tension and anxiety.

It is no longer reasonable to consider sanity and satisfaction without paying some attention to diet—and specifically to making it less extreme.

AGGRESSION

I once asked a group of vegetarians what behavior they associated with eating meat. Several replied "aggression." I pointed out that the Japanese—who were not traditionally meat eaters—were historically quite aggressive.* At home, their meatless style of eating had given rise to a host of martial arts: karate, judo, and kendo—all of which represent a controlled form of aggression. So, it appears, it is not just the presence or absence of aggression but the quality of aggressive behavior that is affected by diet.

There is a tale of a great karate master who was somewhat inconspicuously eating in a Japanese roadside teahouse. Three brash young trouble seekers entered the teahouse and, not knowing the master, began to harass him. He took no notice of them. Their rudeness and unpleasantness continued until the moment he stopped eating. Then, to their surprise, he caught a passing fly in flight with his chopsticks. Seeing this, the three men quietly departed from the teahouse.

Rarely do stories of the Wild West describe the resolution of conflict with such subtlety and self-control.

Two Japanese expressions indicate an awareness of the relationship between meat and aggressive behavior. One term is *niku niku shii;* niku is meat, shii is appearance; literally then, niku niku

---

*Today the Japanese eat about one-tenth the amount of meat consumed per capita in the U.S.A.

shii is meat, meat appearance. In fact, it means boastful and violent behavior.

In contrast, the Japanese word for peace and harmony is *wa*. This word is composed of two characters, one symbolizing grain, and the other mouth.[3] Thus, eating centrally rather than in the extreme was seen as being associated with peace and harmony—an observation I have made in people throughout the world.

wa =

grain & mouth

A similar understanding has been a part of Western culture for thousands of years. It was after the great flood of Noah's time that a second dietary prescription for man was presented in the Bible and it included meat (the first occurs at the beginning of Genesis and was discussed in Chapter 4).

And God blessed Noah and his sons and said unto them... every moving thing that liveth shall be for food for you as the green herb have I given you all. Only flesh with the life thereof which is the blood thereof shall ye not eat. *

GENESIS 9:1-4

This change to meat eating brought with it a new consequence in man's relation to the environment.

Previously, prescribing a diet of seed-bearing plants, God bid man to "replenish the earth and subdue it and have dominion over... every living thing."

GENESIS 1:27

---

*Some interpret this to mean no killing, that is, eating only those animal products that do not require the taking of life—dairy food and eggs. Most people believe, however, that it refers to only eating animals that had been properly killed and bled and to prohibiting the eating of blood or the limbs of live animals, as was the custom.

When prescribing a diet including meat, God bid man to "replenish the earth. . . . And the fear *of you and the* dread *of you shall be upon every beast [fowl and fish]. "*

GENESIS 9:1-2

Clearly, there was an early appreciation that meat eating introduces an element of tension into the environment and reduces a natural harmony between living things.

A BIT OF
WHAT YOU FANCY

One expert has written:

The melancholic fact has been observed that all races from the beginning to the present have been cannibals. The practice existed for a variety of reasons: hunger and famine, [or] ridding the tribe of useless members. [4]

It may or may not be instinctive for man to eat his fellows, but eating some meat has been a part of man's behavioral pattern for thousands of years. Usually, however, the frequency and the quantity of meat eaten were far less than what is consumed in the West today. Often meat was used simply to flavor soups, stews and gruel.

Ethologists report that our primate relatives, the baboons and chimpanzees, though primarily vegetarians, will eat meat if it is available to them. [5] However, natural controls, such as predators and limited supply, make their meat eating a rare occurrence. Man has departed from the natural order by altering the natural controls. He has cultivated livestock and eliminated predators, thus ensuring himself a constant and enormous supply of meat. *

---

*According to one estimate, a 70-year-old American male has consumed 150 cattle, 2400 chickens, 225 lambs, 26 sheep, and 310 hogs in his lifetime.

Meat eating is neither good nor bad. It has been especially important at times when vegetable food has been scarce or unavailable; for example, in winter's cold, during wartime or following a natural catastrophe. Though I rarely eat meat, I seldom advise others not to eat it. It all depends on who you are and where and how you live.

The average American eats meat twice a day, 240 pounds of it a year along with 120 pounds of sugar. Such an extreme diet has extreme consequences to the eater, the environment and the rest of mankind.[6] Some of the effects are shown in the table that follows.

PHYSICAL EFFECTS	PSYCHOLOGICAL EFFECTS
Physical hypertension (high blood pressure)	Tension, anxiety
Heart and vascular disease	Increased frustration, stress
Atherosclerosis	Aggression, insensitivity
Stroke	Materialism
	Excessively high need
	Achievement—fear
Digestive disorders, particularly liver, pancreas and large intestine (cancer)	Anger, impatience, anxiety
	Aggression
	Disturbing dreams, insomnia
	Fear
Kidney disease	Fatigue, tiredness
	Reduced sexual vitality
	Fear
Joint disease	Inflexibility
Arthritis	Limited adaptiveness
Offensive wastes and body odors	Negative self-perception
	Embarrassment and guilt
	Disturbed social relations
Premature aging	Fear and anxiety
	Wastefulness, "live for the moment" attitude
Acidosis	

Extreme diets have also contributed to personal hygiene problems. Body odors and waste products are considerably more offensive among meat and dairy eaters than among vegetarians.

Millions of gallons of deodorant, perfume, aftershave and cologne are bought annually to disguise or enhance body odor. For example, 28.6 million gallons of mouthwash and oral scents mask or freshen the breath in America each year.[7] The need for some of these aids can be reduced by eating less animal food and what is required to balance it.

In Western meat-eating societies there is a tendency to perceive the body as dirty and unholy. The "evils of the flesh" is a meat-eater's concept. Bodily functions are also seen as unpleasant, embarrassing, or somewhat defiling. For example, swear words and jokes about feces, excrement, and urine occur frequently in humor and conversation. Similarly, in our culture sex is often treated as lewd. Such perception of bodily functions is much less frequent in the more vegetarian societies of the East.

To summarize, most individuals eating extreme diets consume more concentrated energy than is necessary, economical or healthful. This is expressed in their personal behavior and social relations and in their use of the environment. It is characterized by excessive tension, anxiety and mental and physical dis-ease.

Some exposure to the extremes is a part of a normal, healthy life. When you eat extreme foods:

- Do so in moderation. Maintain a centered diet.
- Select good quality food, with a minimum of chemical additives and preservatives. Livestock today are fed growth stimulants, female hormones, tranquilizers and antibiotics. Often these animals are stressed and diseased. After slaughtering, their flesh is treated with preservatives (eg., nitrates), color-

ants, and taste enhancers... all of which may be passed on to the consumer.

- Be conscious of what you are eating and how it affects your behavior and well-being.

A NOTE ON SMOKING AND DRINKING

Smoking and drinking are often exacerbated by an excessive diet of meat. That's not to say that one needs to stop eating meat in order to stop smoking or to reduce consumption of alcohol. With motivation, one can will oneself to stop. However, as meat is an extreme contractive food, it increases the need to balance in the opposite extreme and cigarettes, alcohol and coffee are frequent choices.

When people stop drinking liquor, but continue to eat meat, they frequently turn to eating sweets in great quantity to make balance. Smokers often make a similar switch to sweets or increased eating (both of which are expansive) when they continue to eat lots of meat and other contractive and salty foods and try to stop smoking.

To my mind, the relation of meat and alcohol is underscored by the fact that I have never seen a vegetarian alcoholic. That's not to say that I suggest alcoholics become vegetarians. I have observed, however, that an appropriate change of diet, along with effective counseling, has helped many drinkers to become more balanced.

An extreme expansive diet can also increase drinking behavior. Several studies have shown that when rats were fed diets high in sugar and refined carbohydrates and deficient in essential nutrients, the rats drank significantly more alcohol than when they were eating a balanced diet.[8] Both alcohol consumption and sugar eating have an addictive property. Both lower blood-sugar level (see page 86). Low blood sugar increases the desire or craving for more alcohol or sugar.

If you want to stop smoking or drinking, a change of diet can help. Markedly reduce, or eliminate, the extreme foods from your diet: that is, cut down on meat, eggs, and salt and eliminate *all* sugar and refined carbohydrates. Increase the amount of moderately expansive food; that is, salads and fresh fruits (especially raw). Try this for 10 days by itself or along with any other stop-smoking or drinking techniques that make sense to you. Thereafter, eat a centered diet of natural foods and remember that extreme contractive food leads to cravings for extreme expansive tastes. Meat attracts sweet ... or smoke or drink.

From food are born all creatures, which live upon food and after death return to food. Food is the chief of all things. It is therefore said to be medicine for all diseases of the body.

The Upanishads

Psychologists have observed that a moderate amount of tension maximizes behavioral performance for a wide range of tasks. However, too much tension (overcontraction) or not enough (overexpansion) reduces effectiveness and pleasure (see illustration). So it is with diet. Too much of either extreme affects behavior and limits performance.

Overcontraction, Overexpansion

Chapter **8**

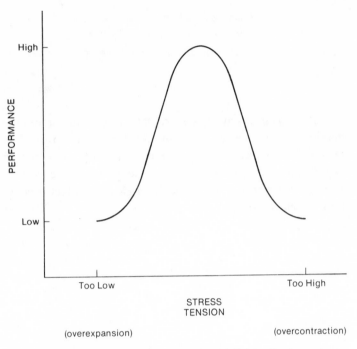

High ┤

PERFORMANCE

Low ┤

Too Low   Too High

STRESS
TENSION

(overexpansion)   (overcontraction)

The "Inverted-U Performance Curve" which Relates Tension and
Stress to Performance

In counseling, I have observed that people with characteristic
attitudes, lifestyle and problems frequently have characteristic
eating habits. Two young couples I counseled are representative.

The first couple were both young executives and recently
married. They were having some difficulty working out their
routines and expectations. They both had clearly defined goals:
they aspired to careers, personal achievement and financial success.
They both had fairly definite and set expectations of what their
partner should and shouldn't do and these were somewhat in
conflict. They both worked hard all day and expected, and wanted,
to come home to an attentive partner, a clean house, and a well-
prepared nourishing dinner, which for them was a steak and a
bottle of wine.

The second couple were "dropouts." They left college pre-
maturely, traveled and had changed their lifestyle considerably.

They became followers of an East Indian sect and then, after a year, left the movement. They were disillusioned and confused and hoped that I might help them to redirect themselves. They had also changed their eating habits and generally followed a vegetarian diet that consisted of large quantities of fruit, yoghurt and honey, with few whole grains.

These couples are in sharp contrast. The first, somewhat rigid with a material orientation and having some trouble reconciling their goals to their partner's needs, were too contracted. The second, without a center, impressionable and drifting, were overexpanded. Along with psychological counseling, there are some very definite changes in diet that would help the first couple to become more flexible, responsive and yielding, and the second couple to become more centered, focused and self-determining.

OVEREXPANSION, OVERCONTRACTION

Having observed that extreme food correlates with extreme behavior, we can now distinguish between the effects on behavior of extreme expansive foods (drugs, sugar, honey and an *excess* of fruits and fruit juices) and of the extreme contractive foods (meat, fish, eggs, cheese and salt).

Extreme expansive food ⟶ Overexpansion
Extreme contractive food ⟶ Overcontraction

These two states of imbalance can be characterized as follows:

Overexpansion. Overexpansion is the state of being too open, or too "spaced out." Thinking may be vague and impractical. Thoughts are sometimes divorced from action and plans, and daydreams are often unrealized.

Overexpansive people frequently lack direction and order. They tend to be too open, too permissive, too expressive and too impressionable. They under-discriminate for their discriminative sense is distorted. They are anxious and often project their thoughts and feelings onto others. They have trouble ordering time and space. Things seem to slip from their grasp, and thus they may appear disorganized, lazy or confused.

Overcontraction. Overcontraction is the state of being too closed, too tense (hypertense) or "uptight." Overcontractive people have great concern and fear of losing control. They continuously attempt to control self, others and situations. They often repress and deny their feelings. They draw boundaries around themselves and can be too discriminating, too withdrawing, too exclusive. As such, they tend to be inflexible and have a reduced ability to empathize and appreciate another's point of view. They also tend to be materialistic, and try to possess, hoard and control people as well as objects.

It's possible, of course, to be something of both, especially if one eats in both extremes. As anything in its extreme turns into its opposite, the end result of overcontraction or overexpansion is virtually the same—a loss of effectiveness (power) and pleasure.

ANXIETY AND ARTHRITIS

Mind and body are one; hence, overcontraction and overexpansion can be expressed throughout the person.

Anxiety is emotional dis-ease. Psychologists and psychiatrists describe it as an irrational fear that underlies neurotic behavior. When anxiety becomes linked with a specific situation, therapists work to dissolve this connection and help the person become more relaxed.

Often the source of anxiety is the internal environment and results from extreme dietary habits. Extreme contractive foods cause tension and loss of flexibility; extreme expansive foods cause overexpansion, disintegration and a similar loss of flexibility and adaptiveness. The end result is the same—an intuitive sense of imbalance; a feeling that something isn't right. Being overcontracted or overexpanded predisposes an individual to tension and anxiety.

Arthritis is joint disease. It may be seen as a condition in which the joints become overcontracted, hardened, tight and inflexible, or overexpanded, inflamed, swollen and inflexible. It only makes sense that along with direct physical therapy (massage, exercise, temperature), a centered diet be advised, that is, a diet free from extreme contractive foods such as meat, eggs, cheese and salt as well as extreme expansive foods such as sugar, wine, acidic fruit juices and chemical additives. This, along with an abstention from fatty foods, is more or less what some arthritis experts advise.

Anxiety and arthritis interact. When the internal environment is disordered, both become activated. When one is stimulated, it in turn stimulates the other. If your arthritis is bothering you, then you're inclined to be tense and anxious. If you are anxious, you tend to become tense and fatigued and experience more discomfort.

The same relationship exists between heart disease and emotional dis-ease. Indeed, many problems can be seen in terms of overcontraction and overexpansion. For all of them, a centered diet with a marked reduction of extreme foods is advised.

In my professional practice, I often teach people how to achieve a state of deep relaxation. Sometimes, relaxation therapy is an adjunct to psychotherapy and counseling; sometimes, relaxation training is preparatory to childbirth.

Like others, I have observed that a diet of extreme foods, especially extreme contractive foods (meat), makes deep relaxation much more difficult. An appropriate alteration in diet makes relaxation training more effective and pleasurable.

DIET AND EXERCISE

It is widely appreciated that exercise is important to our mental and physical well-being. The fundamental function of exercise is to increase the circulation and flow of energy (that is, oxygen, nutrients and electro-chemical impulses) throughout the body. What is often unappreciated, however, is that exercise need not be violent or extreme. Indeed, moderate exercise (with correct body use) is a more efficient and pleasurable way to increase energy flow.

Diet and exercise are inter-related in several ways: (1) Generally, healthy activity increases appetite and improves digestion, and (2) more specifically, certain activities correlate with certain diets and eating patterns. In terms of expansion and contraction, exercise generally has a contractive effect—attracting one to slightly more expansive food. For example, distance running or jogging is a contractive process...one that decreases one's preference for meat (contractive). Traditionally, long-distance and marathon runners ate a high carbohydrate diet of (whole) grains and fruit, a diet that is still reasonable today.*

More extreme (start-stop, bulk-speed) activities usually correlate with more extreme eating habits. For example, an extreme meat and sugar diet is most apt to nurture the violent, explosive, staccato action of competitive, contact sports. I remember the huge breakfasts of orange juice, steak, eggs, honey and coffee that I was fed a few hours before taking the field for a college football game. In contrast, yoga instructors reliably recommend a more

---

*Runners: A centered, natural diet, high in *whole* carbohydrates is recommended for runner and non-runner alike. Sugar leads to unstable performance. The practice of eating lightly, or avoiding solid food, immediately before a race has helped many runners perform better. However, such behaviors as carbohydrate-loading, caffeine-imbibing practiced by some distance runners are stressful and frequently have adverse consequences.

centered diet compatible with the more moderated pace and manner of yoga exercise.*

Extreme food correlates with extreme exercise. However, extreme exercise is not the ideal remedy to an overacid condition produced by excesses of meat, eggs and cheese (contractive foods) on the one hand, and sugar and coffee (expansive foods) on the other. Extreme and violent movement increases circulation and blood flow, but it also produces large quantities of lactic and carbonic acid in a short time period thereby increasing stress and fatigue. What is more beneficial is activity that can be sustained, both during the exercise period (eg. a 45-minute walk) and day to day over the years.

In practical terms, exhausting yourself with violent exercise is extreme and sometimes stressful behavior nurtured by an extreme diet. A more moderate, centered approach to diet and exercise is advised.

A NOTE ON TWO EXTREME NON-FOODS: SALT AND "DRUGS"

Salt. Salt is very contractive. Unlike the foods previously discussed, it is neither animal nor vegetable—it is mineral. Taking salt is one of the few ways we feed directly on the mineral world. Generally, we get the mineral salts we require from the plants and animals we eat. Green vegetables are a rich source of mineral salts. The richest source of natural mineral salts, however, is sea vegetables, or seaweeds. There are 10 to 15 times more minerals in some seaweeds than in an equal weight of beef or trout.

---

*Proper physical exercise and wholesome natural food are two of the five important rules of Yogic health.[1]

Seaweeds were traditionally used in the Americas, Asia, and Europe, and even at times by "primitive" people living far from the sea. Laver (nori), dulse, wakame, kelp (kombu), hiziki and arame are some of the seaweeds available in natural food stores today. They can be used in soups and salads or eaten with grains and vegetables.

The use of sea salt and rock salt is almost universal. The value of salt to mankind is evidenced by its use in language. A good man is said to be "worth his salt," and salary, our term for a daily wage, relates to the practice of payment with salt.

In the past, salt was used both as a preservative and a condiment. Today, it is used by most people to flavor their food. Salt increases saliva flow and may thus facilitate the oral digestion of those foods (like cereal grains) that require a lot of chewing. Salt is also a very extreme substance. As a general rule I avoid adding plain salt at the table. *Occasionally* I use *small* quantities of sesame salt (gomasio), soy sauce or seaweed preparations as condiments. A *little sea salt* or soy sauce may also be used in cooking, but it is not necessary nor should salt be added thoughtlessly or routinely.

Salt has an extreme effect on behavior. This can be observed in those who eat large quantities of salt as well as those who live and work by the sea (fishermen). Prolonged, excessive use of salt can lead to overcontraction, hypertension and rigidity.

> Because of its extremely contractive properties, salt should be used *sparingly* by everyone, especially by those in need of expansion, such as pregnant women or small children, also by those who are already too contracted—those with hypertension (high blood pressure) and the very old.

"Drugs." The most common way of treating mental problems today is by attempting to remove symptoms with drugs. Drugs, *not food,* are being recommended to stimulate, to tranquilize, to remove depression, to wake people up, to help them to sleep, to turn them on and turn them off. Drugs usually have a more intensive

and immediate effect on our biochemistry than food. Many drugs taken are very extreme. Some have a particularly expansive effect on behavior.

The so-called mind-expanding drugs (marijuana and LSD) can induce rapid expansion of consciousness and spark new connections and perceptions. With repeated use, though, these drugs create all the signs of overexpansion—splits between ideas and actions, diffuse thoughts, distorted perception, unrealistic expectations and changes in attitude. The latter are almost always in the direction from active, need-achieving, goal-directed, self-determining, "life's what you make it" to a more passive, uncentered drifting "let it be" attitude...from contraction to expansion.

In counseling university students I have found that one of the most common complaints amongst marijuana smokers is an inability to concentrate or direct attention, as well as a reduced ability to remember or recall material studied. This "cognitive expansiveness" contributes to lower grades and dropping out.*

Since drugs such as marijuana and LSD are very expansive, the people most strongly attracted to them are apt to be those who are material, "uptight" and generally overcontracted. (This is the law of opposites.) This overcontraction is due to many things. It usually follows many years of eating a diet with a high proportion of extreme contractive foods such as meat and eggs. Other contractive influences that cause people to be stressed and uptight are urbanization, crowding and an exaggerated need to achieve.

Sometimes, people are so uptight that therapists recommend expansive drugs to break up their inhibitions and defenses and to help free their emotions. Even under supervision, caution is advised in their use as they are very extreme "foods" with very disintegrating and unbalancing effects that can be both subtle and

---

*These observations were made when the author was a clinical psychologist in counseling and an associate professor of psychology at Mississippi State University.

long-lasting. *This is particularly true for children and adolescents* who
have not developed a strong center or sense of reality. They can
be extremely unbalanced by a protracted period of expansive
drug taking.

If you are "uptight," remember that the most effective and, in
the long run, pleasurable way to make balance is to move into the
center slowly and not to jump into the opposite extreme.

*Man's food is of two worlds, the world above
and the world below.*

We are material and spiritual beings capable of a broad consciousness. Sensitivity to a wide range of stimuli is possible and may be affected by eating certain foods or differing quantities of food. Generally, contractive food and too much food lead to a more weighty, materialistic, and self-centered (centripetal) perception of the world. This is a common phenomenon in our society.

A more expansive diet and abstaining from food for brief periods (fasting) can expand consciousness. Of course overexpansion is also possible. A balanced perception is coincident with a balanced diet.

Balancing
Perspectives

Chapter **9**

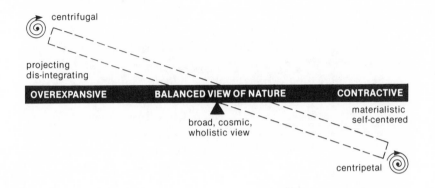

OVEREATING
AND FASTING

Overeating is one way that people reduce their sensitivity. Overeating limits the opportunity to experience the environment in less material ways. If you are full of food, you are simply less open and less able to attract other energy forms.

People often overeat when they are looking for something not found in their food. It is not an uncommon practice to reduce certain feelings by eating excessively. Some people unconsciously eat more than they need to in an attempt to stop feeling empty, lonely, bored or frightened. Overeating can fill you up, dull you, bring you down or turn you off.

> If you are feeling disoriented, confused or dissatisfied, one way to make balance is to eat less; specifically less extreme food.

You can experiment for yourself by simply going without food for a day or two and observing how this affects your thoughts and feelings. After fasting a few days, I experienced what many people have reported—a greater sense of clarity, lightness and awareness. People have also noted with some surprise that the quantity of food they normally consume is far in excess of what they require. (Though it is not recommended without preparation and guidance, most of us could go without any food for a couple of weeks.)

Fasting is not a way of life. It is only a short-term exercise. It is a powerful medicine that allows the body to eliminate excesses, tensions and dis-ease.[1] Many curative and religious doctrines prescribe fasting as a highly effective treatment for all kinds of mental and physical disorders.

And it was by the bed of a stream, many sick fasted and prayed... for seven days and seven nights. And great was their reward... with the passing of the seventh day, all their pains left them.[2]

THE GOSPEL OF PEACE OF JESUS CHRIST

There is also an account of Christ healing a young man who was totally incapacitated by what today would be considered an extreme mental disorder. His disciples were unable to help the man.

And when he was come into the house, his disciples asked him privately, "Why could we not cast him out?" And he said unto them, "This kind can come forth by nothing, but by prayer and fasting."

MARK 9:28-29

A few food-conscious psychiatrists in North America and the Soviet Union have fasted their patients for varying lengths of time to help them to reintegrate and make balance. Many people regularly fast for short periods (a day or so every month) because they find fasting helps them to feel better.

If you are eating a balanced, centered diet, fasting is not necessary. However, fasting does increase clarity and what's becoming clearer to many is that supervised fasting can be an effective short-term remedy for behavioral, emotional and physical imbalance.

FASTING
FOR AWARENESS

Fasting can also broaden perspectives and heighten spiritual awareness. The relationship of fasting to spiritual discovery is described in biographical accounts of Moses, Jesus, Buddha, St. Patrick, Mohammed, and others. Even today, it is standard practice for those seeking Communion to abstain from food or to reduce the quantity of food they eat.

Religious fasts may last a day, as in the Christian fast of Good Friday or the Jewish fast of Yom Kippur; for several days, as in the vision quest of the American Indian; or as long as one month in Ramadan, the annual Moslem holiday during which one does not eat from sunrise to sunset.

Fasting need not be an abstention from all food. Vegetarian fast periods have been established to heighten spiritual awareness.* Orthodox Christians avoid all animal foods twice annually for the 40 days prior to Christmas and Easter. During these fasts, meat, fish, eggs and dairy are all avoided. These contractive foods were thought to stimulate the passions and preoccupy the mind with material thoughts. Fast days were days for creating inner peace and increasing the opportunity for spiritual communion.

Some religious teachers have described the path to spiritual awakening as becoming more accessible after eliminating flesh foods from the diet. Perhaps the most comprehensive treatise on the effect of meat eating on spiritual consciousness was written in the third century by the Greek Porphyry.† According to his observations, liberation from the burdens of flesh eating freed man from base motivations and physical and mental disease. It also "procured for us peace by imparting salvation to our reason

---

*For example, see Chapter 1 of the Book of Daniel.

†Many of the famed Greek spiritual teachers were vegetarians, including Pythagoras, Plato, Socrates, Ovid, Plutarch, Diogenes and Cicero.

power."[3] He went on to point out that the Epicureans, men who thought that pleasure is the end, achieved this state not through gormandizing and gluttony (as is commonly believed), but on a *simple* diet of maize and fruit.

DREAM FOOD

Food is functional. It fills a stomach and a need. People with different needs, goals and dreams select and require different foods. The prize fighter and the yogi eat a different diet.

Over the centuries, the sages and yogis of India developed a dietary code based on their *experience* of the effects of food on their health, behavior and spiritual practice. The Hindu scriptures (the *Bhagavad Gita*) described all things, including food and behavior, in terms of three qualities (gunas)—sattvic, rajasic, and tamasic. In the *Bhagavad Gita* it states:

> *The foods which increase vitality, energy, vigor, health, and joy and which are delicious, bland, substantial, and agreeable are dear to the pure. The passionate persons desire foods that are bitter, sour, saline, excessively hot, pungent, dry, and burning, and which produce pain, grief, and disease. The food which is stale, tasteless, putrid, rotten, and impure is dear to the Tamasic.*

Sattvic (pure) foods are centered foods. They nurture a stable, sensitive, sattvic mentality...one that enables an individual to live harmoniously with "the mind pure and calm." They are uplifting foods; sweet and bland-tasting foods. Sattvic foods include whole grains (rice, wheat, barley), fruits, leafy vegetables and milk.

Rajasic (stimulating) foods are extreme foods with an unsettling effect on the nervous system and behavior. They heighten the emotions, "excite passion and make the mind restless, unsteady, and uncontrollable."[4] Rajasic foods include salt, spices, meats, alcohol, sugar, coffee and some root vegetables (eg. onions, garlic, radish).

Tamasic (impure) foods are those foods which are stale, putrid or rotten. They have the effect of lowering consciousness, and increasing disturbing thoughts, depression, inertia and disease. Tamasic foods include fermented drinks (beer, wine), readily spoiled meats (pork), tomatoes and tobacco.

The yogis were the scientists of their day. Their observations of the effects of various foods were based on a sensitivity developed through diet, exercise, meditation and breathing techniques rather than sophisticated laboratory equipment or biofeedback devices.

A yogi, a gymnast, a dancer, a meditator, a performer or anyone who has sensitized him- or herself through practice and discipline becomes aware of how many factors, including food, affect their health and performance.

Feedback is essential to sound judgement and development. Through living and eating in a sane and balanced manner each of us can become aware of which foods increase our well-being and which help us to realize our dreams.

IT'S NOT JUST FOOD

For most people, feeling lighter and more spiritually alive is more than a matter of "eating well." That's just the beginning. Under natural circumstances, spiritual development usually takes time, guidance and the disciplined practice of certain activities. To satisfy these conditions, some have sought the seclusion of religious orders. The same principles apply to anyone, however, anywhere at any age. They are activity, a simple diet and a little self-reflection.

I once asked a British friend, who was a vegetarian, a teacher and an author, what diet she advised for a balanced perception of life. What is most important, she said, is that you eat foods that are wholesome and that you enjoy, and that your attitude toward your food is grateful and receptive. When one feels it is appropriate for spiritual growth and development to stop eating flesh, it will be time for him or her to give up these foods. She does not recommend that anyone impose a diet on him- or herself that is alien to his or her wishes. Restriction only breeds resentment.[5]

ROOTS

Almost every tradition has teachings about food—about what and how to eat and what to avoid. Many of these teachings have since been forgotten, fragmented, distorted, or practiced with limited understanding.

You might explore the dietary teachings and traditions of your religious faith or ethnic background. See what directions they provide for improving your physical, mental and spiritual well-being and for increasing your conscious awareness.

A NATURAL PERSPECTIVE

Proteins, carbohydrates and fats are *not foods*—they are nutritional categories that can be difficult to relate to. Everyone's familiar with apples, oranges, eggs, fish, bread and nuts. There is some confusion, though, about how much protein, carbohydrates and fats we ''should'' eat and whether proteins are good, and carbohydrates bad.

The recommended daily quantities of protein, carbohydrates and fats vary between experts and countries. About the only *natural perspective* we have as to the appropriate relative proportions of

these nutrients is from the composition of mother's milk—the
perfect food for human *infants* (see the following table).

Mother's milk consists of approximately:*	In contrast, the average American consumes a diet of:
8–10% protein	12–14% protein
26–29% fat	37–42% fat
65% carbohydrate	47–55% carbohydrate

*The actual numbers vary somewhat with the diet and constitution of
the mother.

While the requirements for infants and adults may not be the
same, the significantly higher percentages of fat and protein in the
diet of most adults may be a major cause of overweight as well as
of mental and physical disease.

Protein. The primary function of protein is the synthesis of body
protein and new cells. It follows that infants experiencing more
rapid growth and development would require as much if not more
protein than adults. The 8 to 10 percent protein in human milk is
in keeping with the finding that 8 to 10 percent of an infant's total
calorie consumption is used for the formation of new tissue and
growth.[6] It is also in keeping with the 7:1 carbohydrate:protein
ratio discussed earlier (page 16). Today, in the more affluent
countries, the average adult is consuming 25 to 35 percent more
protein than what Mother Nature provides for infants. An excessive
consumption of high protein (contractive) foods increases stress.
It produces more uric acid and toxic wastes and requires large
quantities of fluid (expansive) as well as expansive foods to make
balance.

Fats. The consumption of fats by most Westerners, consisting of
over 40 percent of their diets, is *far* in excess of what is natural and
healthful. This significant overconsumption of fat has been linked
to many diseases including heart and vascular diseases, cancer,

diabetes, senility and deafness. The recommendations for dietary change by heart sufferers are typically insufficient and unrealistic —about 35 percent fat.[7] Dietary fat content should rarely exceed 30 percent in *healthy* individuals.

Carbohydrates. Carbohydrates form the bulk of the human diet. They represent a wide range of substances containing carbon, hydrogen and oxygen. Many people think that carbohydrates are not good for them. They lump together in this category whole grains, vegetables, fruits with sugar, ''sweets'' and pastry. The former are the basis of a healthy diet; the latter are causes of stress and disease (see the next two chapters). Whole, unrefined carbohydrates should constitute over 60 percent of most people's diets. Today, however, people are eating less carbohydrates and about 33 percent of the carbohydrates they do consume comes from sugar.

I prefer to talk to people about food rather than nutritional categories like proteins, carbohydrates and fats. In my experience, information on food is more easily communicated and put to use. To maintain a balanced perspective, nutritional standards and advice should be in harmony with natural patterns and processes.

Natural food ⟶ *natural behavior. However, eating "unnaturally" has become a way of life for most Americans and Europeans. By eating "unnaturally," I mean eating foods that have been refined and chemically processed; eating foods more appropriate to infants; eating fatty foods; and just plain eating too much. These patterns are all unnatural and uncentering and can lead to disorder.*

In this section, I describe how unnatural eating can lead to unnatural behavior and explain how to eat more naturally.

EATING UNNATURALLY

Section **III**

Man has long understood that whole is beautiful. Hale, wholesome and hearty are terms that reflect a well-being that comes through wholeness and integration. It has been said, "They that are whole need not a physician" (Matthew 9:12).

Within every plant or animal, there is a dynamic balance of energy. Removing or separating out the parts disturbs energy flow and balance and destroys the natural vitality of the substance. Eating un-whole foods, those that have been refined or disintegrated, appears to affect us in the same way.

The foods most affected are those most frequently refined—the carbohydrates, especially grains and sugars. Since our "daily bread" is now disintegrated, it should come as no surprise that symptoms of physical and mental disintegration are widespread.

Dis-Integration

Chapter **10**

I am sometimes asked: "If disintegrated food leads to disintegrated behavior, doesn't refined food lead to refined behavior?" The answer is "No." Refined carbohydrates cannot support life and must be supplemented (by animal foods, fiber or bran and vitamins). A diet of refined carbohydrates and animal foods is a diet of affluence, but it is also a diet associated with physical and mental disorder.

It has been reliably reported that when "primitive peoples" around the world (e.g., Eskimos, Yemenite Jews, Polynesians, and Zulus) become "civilized" and adopt a diet of refined carbohydrates, there is a marked increase in their physical and mental disorders.[1] Conversely, when limited food supplies during famine or wartime make it impossible to eat a diet of refined foods, certain disorders disappear in spite of the fact that stress factors increase. For example, during the Second World War, when the British and Scandinavians were forced to eat more wholemeal breads and grains and less meat and refined foods, there was a marked reduction in certain intestinal and mental disorders.[2]

One of the pioneers of nutritional research spent several years living with the Hunzas (a Himalayan people). On the basis of his experience, he was led to the conclusion that diet was the outstanding factor responsible for the marked superiority of the Hunzas over the rest of the native population. Their diet was primarily whole grain cereals along with some local vegetables, fruit and a little dairy food. Refined flour, sugar and meat were rarely eaten. Meat was only eaten in winter, and then only in very small quantities.

In a classic experiment to verify the significance of a whole food diet for overall well-being, one group of rats was fed a diet typical of the Hunzas (primarily whole grains), while two other groups of rats were fed a diet typical of parts of India and the British lower class (refined carbohydrates including sugar, tea, spices and a little milk). The rats fed the Hunza diet thrived, grew and mated normally. They had healthy offspring and manifested no ills. The rats fed the refined food diets soon acquired a host of diseases: pneumonia, anemia, sinusitis, ulcers, goiter, heart disease and premature birth.

What is perhaps more interesting from a psychological viewpoint is that the temperament of the Hunza rats was gentle, playful and affectionate; they got on well with each other and with their handlers. The temperament of the refined food rats, on the other hand, was described as irritable and vicious.*

Since these early discoveries, a variety of human disorders have been reported to be associated with eating refined foods.[4] The list includes:

- ulcers, tumors and cancer of the large intestine
- heart and vascular disease (including varicose veins)
- gall stones, appendicitis and hemorrhoids
- diabetes and hypoglycemia
- obesity
- tooth and gum disease

as well as psychotic behavior, anxiety, apathy, depression, and uncontrollable, violent and anti-social behavior.

Many of these conditions improve drastically when refined foods are eliminated from the person's diet.

FIBER AND BEHAVIOR

One reason psychological well-being is adversely affected by eating refined foods is that the gastro-intestinal system is intimately connected with the coordinating and integrating mechanisms of the nervous system. Non-specific nerve fibers ("C" fibers) which are dispersed throughout the entire length of the intestines conduct impulses from the intestines to the "arousal" center of the brain

---

*This classic study expresses the pattern of feeding human diets to animals and extrapolating from the findings to the effect of food on man.[3] This approach makes any study of the *subtle* effects of our food on our personality almost impossible.

(the reticular activating system). This energy input primes the central nervous system and facilitates the effective conduction of *all* incoming and outgoing messages.

When you eat whole high-fiber foods, there is a rapid, continuous, smooth transit of food through your intestines. This leads to a regular continuous firing of the non-specific nerve fibers into your arousal system and more effective neuronal conduction. The manifest result is more integrated and coordinated behavior.

In contrast, when you eat a refined or low-fiber diet (lots of white flour, sugar and meat), "transit times" of food through the intestines are increased several times. Slow transit times are associated with interrupted, discontinuous intestinal activity and more generally with tension and disease. The discontinuous, irregular activity of the intestines leads to an asynchronous, irregular firing of the non-specific nerve fibers into the arousal system. This, in turn, promotes unreliable and ineffective neuronal conduction which is expressed as disintegrated behavior.

An even more basic reason why eating refined foods leads to disordered behavior is that refined foods promote incomplete, inefficient digestion with slow transit times and *the accumulation of toxins*. This is especially true for those eating a diet of meat, eggs, cheese and refined carbohydrates. With slow transit times, the animal foods putrify in the intestines producing toxic byproducts, which, if not quickly eliminated, cause biochemical and behavioral disorders.* Anxiety, aggression and depression may all be nurtured in this manner.

WHAT ABOUT BRAN?

The significance of fiber in the diet and the dangers of refining food are becoming popular knowledge. One British physician

---

*Unlike the carbohydrates (which consist of carbon, hydrogen and oxygen) a characteristic feature of proteins is that they contain nitrogen. It is the nitrogenous properties of protein food wastes that render them particularly toxic and stressful to the organism and demand their rapid elimination.

spoke on fiber at a wholefood conference I attended in England. He reported the finding that eating *whole* food, especially whole grain, substantially reduced many disorders. Like many experts, he suggested that eating wheat bran could provide the necessary ingredient missing in disintegrated diets. His presentation included slides of patients being treated in a hospital. Some of the slides showed a group of men "taking their medicine"—spoonfuls of bran—but continuing to eat white bread and other refined foods.

This is, of course, a disintegrated way of dealing with the problems of disintegration, but many people are attempting to do just that. They are putting bran in or on everything, and then continuing to eat *refined* foods. Some pharmaceutical firms are even manufacturing synthetic bran which is sold as medicine to people needing roughage in their diet.

There is no question that bran provides an increase of fiber to the diet and promotes faster transit times and greater regularity. Bran is not a whole food, however, nor is it a substitute for whole food. The dynamic balance within food is lost when it is refined and bran cannot replace that.

Adding bran to *whole* food is unnecessary. Some whole-food eaters even tell me it upsets them. Experiment for yourself. If you find that it increases your sense of well-being, then by all means use it. I recommend that it not be used as a substitute for whole food.

WHAT ABOUT VITAMINS?

The vitamin story is similar to that of fiber. Next to food shortage, the single greatest cause of vitamin deficiency is the massive refinement and processing of food. The dynamic vitality and vitamins in food are destroyed with processing.*

---

*The graph shows the relation of extraction rate (refinement) and the proportion of vitamins retained by the grain (wheat flour).[5] With the standard extraction rate for most breads (about 65 percent), *at least half* (50 percent) of the vitamin content of the flour is lost.

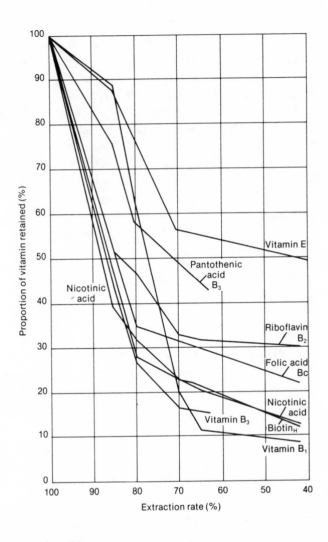

Whole grains are naturally rich in the B vitamins and vitamin E—substances linked to healthy mental function and sexual behavior.[6] In the process of converting whole wheat into *white* bread, the following natural vitamins may be lost:

Vitamin B₁ (thiamin)	90% lost
Vitamin B₂ (riboflavin)	70% lost
Vitamin B₃ (niacin, nicotinic acid)	70% lost
Vitamin B₆ (pyrodoxine)	80% lost
Other B complex vitamins lost include:	
Panothenic acid	50% lost
Folic acid	70% lost
Biotin	80% lost
Vitamin E	50% lost

While bread may be "enriched" with synthetic vitamins, the quantity and quality of these vitamins is in no way equal to what was removed in processing.

Vitamin deficiency has been linked with a host of mental disorders including anxiety, hyperactivity, delusions, psychotic episodes, depression and mental retardation. Some experts have advised vitamins to overcome these deficiencies.[7] What this means is that vitamins, the essences of substances (e.g., the B vitamins niacin and thiamine extracted from their original source, *whole* grain) are administered in an attempt to regulate a biochemical imbalance that was often caused or exacerbated by eating refined foods in the first place. Frequently, vitamins are advised without any changes in diet.

In megavitamin therapy, massive doses of vitamins are employed. There are some reports that this is an effective way of dealing with drug and alcohol psychosis—psychochemical imbalances caused by extreme and disintegrated "foods," as well as some forms of psychotic-like behavior in children.[8] The results are still controversial. Vitamin therapy may prove an effective *adjunct* to treatment in some extreme instances, but as a general rule vitamins are unnecessary when people eat a centered, balanced diet of natural *whole* food (see page 99).

What is essential exists in natural whole food in appropriate proportion. When you eat refined foods such as sugar and alcohol, your body will deplete its own reserves of vitamins and minerals in order to metabolize these substances. This is both unbalancing and disintegrating.

OUR DAILY BREAD

Almost one-third of the whole grain is lost in the milling of white flour along with most of the vitamins and minerals. This is a wasteful and disruptive process for our daily bread. In the recent past, white bread was a food for special occasions. Today it is an everyday filler.

In England and America, only about 5 percent of the bread sold is called wholemeal and many of the breads labeled as 100 percent natural wholewheat bread are neither whole nor as wholesome as advertised. Anyone can observe the properties of these new breads by giving them a look, a squeeze and a taste.

The availability on the supermarket shelves of many complex, refined and processed foods along with the virtual absence of simple whole food is a measure of socio-economic disintegration. It also undermines our health. As one writer put it,

What do I find wrong with America?. . . I begin at the beginning with the staff of life, bread. If the bread is bad, the whole of life is bad. Bad? Rotten, I should say. Like that piece of bread only twenty-four hours old which is good for nothing except perhaps to fill up a hole. [9]

Today's daily bread is incomplete and the commercial re-fortified breads are just not the same as wholemeal. Compare the difference for yourself. Take a slice of real whole wheat bread and chew it until each piece dissolves completely in your mouth. Count the total number of chews and observe how the taste changes as you chew. Now repeat this exercise with a piece of enriched white bread.

One day, I asked a group of fifty college students to do just that. Each student was given four equal-sized pieces of white and wholemeal bread. (Order of presentation was controlled.) The students were asked to observe their behavior with regard to the number of chews and changes in taste. The wholemeal bread required more chewing than did the white (wholemeal, 49 chews per piece; white, 36).[10] Perhaps more significant, however, was the unanimous report that the wholemeal bread became tastier the more it was chewed while the white bread did not change favorably with increased chewing.

Wholemeal bread requires more chews, and it encourages (reinforces) this behavior by becoming tastier with increased chewing.

CHEWING

Chewing is not simply a medium for comparison, but an important part of the digestive process and *the one over which we have the greatest conscious control.* All behaviors reflect the energy of the whole. The way people chew food is an indication of how they live their lives. Some people bolt their food, others take their time, some take small bites, others bite off more than they can chew. These response tendencies carry over into daily life.

The founder of Gestalt psychotherapy noted that many adults treat solid food as if it were liquid to be swallowed in gulps without chewing. He observed that such individuals are usually characterized by impatience, demands for immediate gratification and an inability to achieve satisfaction. Just as they haven't the patience to chew real food, so they do not take sufficient time to chew mental food. They readily and indiscriminately accept what they're told, and like children swallow things too easily.[11]

Chewing is a multi-functional process. Mechanically it helps to break up food and increase its surface area, enabling chemicals in the saliva to begin the digestion of starches. Chewing also stimulates the flow of gastric juices.

Psychologically, chewing is relaxing and integrating. Chewing stimulates the parasympathetic nervous system, which in turn stimulates the digestive system. As such, chewing is a meditation, one which harmonizes the body and prepares it to receive food. The work of a British psychologist suggests that the way we eat may reflect our sexual behavior. While conducting research on couples with psychosexual problems, he found that slow, careful eaters scored significantly higher ratings as sensualists in bed than did those who ate quickly and mechanically (M. Yaffee, London, 1979).

Chewing also provides a normal healthy outlet for our agression. Many people who don't chew their food thoroughly grind their teeth unconsciously. This behavior (bruxism) is often an expression of excessive tension and unresolved aggression. "By chewing our food well...aggression is thereby put to work in its proper biological place. It is neither sublimated, nor exaggerated, nor is it suppressed, therefore it harmonizes (the individual) with his (or her) personality."[12]

Eating (whole) foods that require more chewing, and chewing them well, can be relaxing and integrating and can improve your health and digestion.

Scientists have observed the adverse effects of sugar on mankind for over one hundred years. Yet, refined and purified of its nutrients, sugar is forming an increasingly large part of most people's diets. In the process, it is replacing important nutrients, depleting vitamins and minerals and affecting behavior.

The average American (and Englishman) consumes over 120 pounds of sugar per year. Sugar is found in most processed foods; even in the non-sweet ones such as soups, breakfast cereals, white bread, mayonnaise, salad dressing, canned vegetables, many "health foods", cigarettes, some cheeses, beer and baby foods.

Sugar

Chapter **11**

People often tell me that they don't use sugar, unaware of the considerable amounts they consume unconsciously as part of their daily fare. It has been estimated that as much as *70 percent* of the sugar that Americans consume is not eaten directly, but hidden in the processed and unnatural foods that they eat.

Books have been written about the destructive properties of this disintegrating food.[1] Its effects are not confined to any one system, but influence circulation (heart and vascular disease), digestion (from tooth decay to hemorrhoids), locomotion (arthritis) and the nervous system (disordered behavior).

SUGAR AND BEHAVIOR

Most people know that sugar is tasty and that tasty foods are usually nourishing. Yet sugar, and most sugar substitutes, have almost no nutritive value. Eating any food with so marked a taste and such little nutritional consequence is bound to be disorienting.

Generally, your reaction to the taste of (natural) food serves as an indicator of your desire or need for that food. However, when sugar is added to a food to make it "taste better," it masks or distorts the original taste. Eating sweetened food can thus distort your discriminative sense and desensitize you to your food. In the end, it may support and even encourage your eating food that you don't require or even desire.

INTO THE MOUTHS OF BABES

Children and adolescents are the prime sugar consumers and it is no wonder. The practice of putting sugar in baby foods and formulas is particularly disrupting for it affects the child in its formative years when it is acquiring its earliest eating habits.

You can observe the effects of sugar eating in children at play. There is often an initial manic stage when children display nervousness and difficulty in sticking to a task as well as loud, high-pitched vocalizations such as shrieking and screaming. This is accompanied by considerable non-specific (non-goal-directed) energy, incessant movement and fidgeting. A depressive stage characterized by whining or crying and complaint usually follows. During this period, total body movement may decrease, but a restless peripheral movement of hands and feet may still be present.

Sugar disintegration may bring with it an identification with something other than oneself, thus nurturing possessiveness and a demand for material objects—"that's mine...I want that...give me." There is more selfish demanding and less of a cooperative sharing ethic. A common response to this unpleasantness is often to bribe the child with a sweet "to be good" and thus the cycle repeats itself.

In some classrooms in the United States and Europe the practice exists of rewarding good school work with candy. Obviously, this is not a wholesome practice. Of course many teachers are aware of the effects of sugar on behavior and are anti-sweet. Some have reported to me that after recess "candy breaks," the children return to the classroom in a more hyperactive and undisciplined state.

In India, I lived for a short time in the home of a poor rural family. In the months that I knew this family it appeared the children never ate sweets or sugar. This is unlike poor families in Europe and North America, who generally consume large amounts of sugar. A treat for this Indian family consisted of some grapes or an orange. If I returned from the village with a surprise, such as roasted chick peas, peanuts, bananas or grapes, the children always divided them up amongst themselves and though plainly excited, left some for the children who were not present. They seemed pleased to share and often offered me a part of some treat given them. They were a mischievous bunch of kids, but I never heard them whine or complain or even act selfishly. Of course there are many factors to account for their behavior, but one of relevance was their centered, natural and *sugarless* diet.

SPOILING CHILDREN

The term "spoiled" with regard to children is inappropriate in that it implies a fixed or irreversible state. However, it does describe a phenomenon. So-called spoiled children are characterized by their demands and expectations, which exist without any apparent means of fulfilling them. Sugar is the perfect spoiling food. It provides an instant sweet taste with little nourishment and without the need for chewing.

Giving sweets to a loved one is a long-time custom...'sweets for the sweet." Sometimes, though, sweets can be a substitute for the direct expression of affection. Once again this is most significant and disintegrating as regards the young who are dependent for their affection as well as their food. Symbols for the source of sweets and affection, "the candy man" and "the sugar daddy," are both purveyors of pleasure and degenerate spoilers. A non-professional appreciation of sugar's degenerative and addictive properties is evidenced by the fact that, in certain circles, both terms have come to mean "the drug pusher."

> Sugar eating is sensory indulgence. It fixes consciousness in the nerve ends and "sensitizes" the sugar-eater to pain. The "sweet life" is one of instability and extremes.

SUGAR DISEASE AND HYPOGLYCEMIA

The physiological effect of eating excessive amounts of refined carbohydrates—especially sugar—is the overproduction of insulin and low blood sugar (hypoglycemia). People often ask why eating sugar and sweets leads to *low* and not high blood sugar.

When you eat sugar, or any carbohydrate, it is converted into a simple sugar which goes into your bloodstream. We can't make use of sugar in this form. What is required is insulin, a substance produced by the pancreas which makes it possible for blood sugar to be absorbed and metabolized by our cells. When too much sugar enters the bloodstream, the pancreas overworks to produce enough insulin to metabolize the sugar. If you regularly eat too much sugar, refined carbohydrates, or just plain overeat, the pancreas "learns" to overproduce insulin. That is, the pancreas (a ductless gland) continuously drips insulin into the bloodstream, gradually reducing the blood-sugar level and eventually lowering it too much. The result is that a couple of hours after eating too sweet or too much, you may experience low blood sugar. In this state, people may feel irritable, fatigued, stressed and hungry. They may want something to eat, and usually it's sugar or something sweet they reach for.

If you then take a pick-me-up sweet, it further stimulates insulin production so that, after an initial rise, blood-sugar level drops even more than before. This is experienced as still more stress, more hunger, and the cycle repeats itself. The sugar-stress cycle with its addictive features is depicted below.

The Sugar-Stress Cycle

If these eating habits continue, the pancreas, overworked and stressed, slows or stops insulin production. The result is high blood sugar, sugar in the urine and even diabetes.

Blood-sugar imbalance has definite marked psychological concomitants. It has been linked to extreme and sudden shifts in mood, mania, depression, anxiety, indecision, distorted body image and confusion. Low blood-sugar level alone has reportedly been a cause of apathy, indifference and "the blues" on the one hand and uncontrollable emotional outbursts and violence on the other.[2]

One reason why sugar has disastrous effects on human behavior is that the nervous system uses a kind of simple sugar (glucose) as its fuel. Special cells in the brain (the glucoreceptors of the hypothalamus) continually monitor and regulate the amount of glucose in the blood. If it is deficient, sugar stored in the body is released and converted into glucose. If it is in excess, insulin is released, which helps to metabolize the excess sugar. This very sensitive and vital process *is intimately linked to what we eat.*

Generally, the more expansive foods have a more unbalancing or upsetting effect on blood-sugar level and behavior. Aside from sugar, such "foods" as coffee, tea, cola, alcohol, tobacco and expansive drugs all have a marked effect on blood-sugar level and behavior.

Caffeine, which is found in coffee, tea, cola drinks and chocolate, is a stimulant which stimulates the adrenal glands to produce epinepherine. Epinepherine, in turn, stimulates the pancreas to secrete insulin, thus lowering blood-sugar level. One cup of coffee or tea, two cokes, four ounces of bitter chocolate, or one stay-awake pill all contain over 75 milligrams of caffeine...enough to cause noticeable blood-sugar and behavioral changes in many adults. The nicotine found in tobacco stimulates epinepherine production in a similar manner. This, in turn, over-stimulates the pancreas and, the result is that blood-sugar level is suppressed. Alcoholic beverages affect the pancreas somewhat more directly, upsetting blood-sugar level and carbohydrate metabolism.

The dramatic effect of expansive drugs like marijuana on blood-sugar level is reliably experienced as excessive hunger and/ or cravings, particularly for sweets. In all cases blood-sugar changes produced by sweet or non-sweet expansive foods increase emotional liability (see page 88).

CARBOHYDRATES CAN BE DIFFERENT

The term "carbohydrate" represents a wide variety of foods, not all of which affect us in the same way. For example, when we eat whole grains they are broken down slowly into simple sugars at a rate which can be readily absorbed and metabolized by the body; a rate that leads to *stable* behavior. Vegetables and fruits are broken down more quickly; their sugar is more readily available. Large quantities of fruit and fruit juice can cause sugar excesses and imbalance along with swings in mood and some emotional instability. The carbohydrate that most upsets the nervous system and behavior is sugar. When sugar (white or brown) is eaten, there is an immediate disruptive effect on the whole organism. Blood-sugar level rises rapidly and then is quickly and significantly depressed. This process has direct and immediate expression in

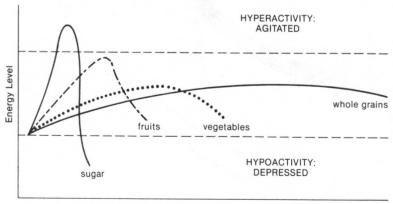

The Relationship of Carbohydrate Metabolism to Behavioral Stability

The Relationship of Sugar Availability to Emotional Liability (Instability)

EXPANSIVE

"drugs"

liquor

beer, wine

sugar, syrups

coffee, tea

fruit juice

EXTREME FOODS

grapes (bunch)
melon, citrus
apple, pear
berry, cherry
fruits

lettuce, spinach
cabbage, celery
roots, carrots
vegetables

milk

CENTERED FOODS

oats, buckwheat
wheat, barley
rice
corn (maize)
cereal grains

Sugar Availability

Emotional Liability

the nervous system, the endocrine system and behavior. With prolonged and/or repeated sugar eating, all three become chronically disordered.

As you can see from the graph on page 87, sugar can cause extreme and unstable behavior—both hyperactive and hypoactive behavior. In many cases, an initial stage of hyperactivity and agitation is followed by a period of hypoactivity and depressed activity.

Blood-sugar imbalance correlates with a wide variety of behavioral symptoms, including:

DEPRESSION	AGITATION	ERRATIC BEHAVIOR
depression	anxiety	irrational behavior
drowsiness	excitability	blackout
fatigue	impatience	confusion, indecision
lethargy	insomnia	delusion
listlessness	irritability	disorientation
whining, crying	nervousness	inability to concentrate
"the blues"	tantrums	memory lapses
		violent outbursts

Sugar may also disrupt behavior by having an inhibitory effect on neurotransmission. A recent finding suggests that sugar reduces the availability of certain substances from which the brain makes many of its neurotransmitters (chemical compounds that carry information from neuron to neuron in the brain).[3] The end result is the same—sugar leads to disintegrated behavior.

WHAT TO DO FOR YOUR SWEET TOOTH

The strong attraction that many people have to sweets is, to a large extent, a function of their excessive consumption of meat, fish, eggs, cheese and salt. This is the law of opposites—meat attracts sweet. It should also be clear that sugar itself can reduce blood-sugar level is best avoided. Simply reducing these foods reduces the craving for sweets.

My sweet tooth has almost disappeared over the years since I started eating a centered diet of whole foods and avoiding the extremes of meat and sugar. Now, if I want something sweet, fresh fruit is sufficient; I find sugar and candy much too sweet. I have also noticed that when I do eat fish or an egg, I get a stronger craving for sweets and a small quantity of fruit often isn't enough to satisfy me.

I generally advise people to eliminate sugar (white or brown) from their diet. Sugar substitutes and artificial sweeteners have some similar effects to sugar. They are disintegrating and desensitize the individual to his needs by distorting the natural taste of foods. Some of them (cyclamates and saccharin) have been the cause of serious illness in laboratory animals. These and similar chemical foods are best avoided.

Many people use honey as a sugar substitute. Wild honey is an extremely powerful food. One teaspoon may represent thousands of flower visits. As such, it seems inappropriate to eat it liberally for its sweet taste. Used sensibly, it is a medicine, a stimulant for growth, activity and revitalization. Used regularly, its effects diminish. Honey (like molasses, sorgum and maple syrup) is a very expansive food and can contribute to many of the same behaviors as does sugar.

In my opinion, the question, "What can I eat to satisfy my sweet tooth?" is best answered with another question: "How can I eat to reduce my need for sweets?"

A NOTE ON CRIMINAL BEHAVIOR

There has been surprisingly little research on the effects of food on criminal behavior, yet the increase of crime in America and Europe correlates almost perfectly with the rise in consumption of extreme and disintegrating foods. Low blood sugar, which is becoming widespread, has been directly correlated with all sorts of criminal behavior. The list includes assault, arson, murder, robbery and vandalism. In one Argentinian study, blood-sugar tests were taken on a group of one hundred and twenty-nine apprehended delinquents. Only thirteen were reported to have had blood sugars within the normal limits.[4]

A functional relationship between nutrition and criminal behavior has also been observed by an Ohio probation officer. She noted that 82 percent of 102 probationers reported fifteen symptoms of hypoglycemia, with some having 50 or more symptoms. Once these individuals were placed on a corrective diet, free from sugar and refined carbohydrates, they exhibited a marked improvement in their attitude towards themselves and society. Results with adult probationers have been so successful that the program is now being extended to juvenile offenders.[5]

Similarly, marital conflicts and domestic violence (wife and child beating) have been linked to diet and blood-sugar levels, as have self-destructive acts, suicide and "accidental" aggression (e.g., car and hunting accidents).[6]

Criminal rehabilitation provides an excellent opportunity to reeducate dietary habits. But this is not being done. The traditional prison diet was essentially coarse wholemeal bread or gruel. In sufficient quantities and supplemented by fresh greens, vegetables and fruits, *it is a centering diet and one that nurtures a change of perspective.* Today, prison diets are uncentered and unbalanced with a high proportion of extreme and disintegrated food.

Visiting prisons in the United States and Canada, I was amazed at the lack of common sense and direction in their rehabilitative programs. Throughout there was a lack of discipline, controlled stimulation and a healthy diet. These conditions often existed in spite of new and sophisticated rehabilitative technology and techniques and increased "prisoner's rights." In one United States federal penitentiary, I watched male offenders in weird costumes of their own choosing, their appearances unkempt, sitting around playing cards and drinking cokes in the middle of the afternoon. The prison psychiatrist informed me that they didn't have to work and they didn't have to have therapy.

A well-known American personality wrote:

As a veteran occupant of some of the nation's most prestigious jails, I think the jails and prisons of America would be a perfect place to initiate dietary reform and nutritional rehabilitation. In the jails are many addicts and others suffering from mental disturbance and emotional hostilities which could be corrected by dietary reform. [7]

He goes on to advocate an increase in fresh fruit, vegetables and salads and a marked reduction of meat, candies and pastries (extreme foods). Fasting and an educational program in nutrition and self-care are also suggested.

Not only might changes of this kind reduce recidivism (now approximately 75 percent) and the overall medical and food expenditure, but they would provide a basic medium for change... a healthy biochemistry.

Over four thousand years ago it was written:

Those who rebel against the basic rules of the universe sever their own roots and ruin their true selves . . . the two principles in nature (expansion and contraction) and the four seasons are the beginning and the end of everything and they are also the cause of life and death. Those who disobey the laws of the universe will give rise to calamities and visitations while those who follow the laws of the universe remain free from dangerous illness.

THE YELLOW EMPEROR'S
CLASSIC OF INTERNAL MEDICINE[1]

Alienation

Chapter **12**

We are composed of the same energy as our environment and are subject to the same rhythms that affect it. Alienation is a lack of attunement or sensitivity to these patterns. It is a form of disintegration between man and his environment. For most people, it involves adopting unnatural rhythms with an increasing reliance on technology to keep ordered, to tell the time, the weather, to determine their feelings or the state of their health. Diet is a factor contributing to this behavior.

Alien foods are those which are not a part of our natural environment. At one time, this referred to foods that were out of season or from faraway regions. Traditional and practical teachings from the Far East (Tao, Zen), the Middle East (Essene), Europe (Salernum) and early America have all advocated, "Eat what is in season in the land in which you live."[2]

Food is an expression of the environment and eating seasonally and regionally is a straightforward way of keeping in harmony and thus reducing disorder and disease. For example, in summertime, when it is warm, expansive foods such as fruits and leafy vegetables allow us to be more open and stay cool. In cold weather, a slightly more contractive diet (more grains, beans, animal food, less fruit) enables us to conserve our heat and energy more effectively. That is, to be more contractive.

As we exercise greater control over our environment, our living and eating patterns change. Some of these changes are not drastic and seem to make life more comfortable but even these can be alienating. For example, with central heating, people in cold northern regions can relax at home in mid-winter wearing summer clothing and oblivious to the cold outside. Many eat tropical foods regularly. The problem that develops when people eat *large* quantities of oranges, bananas, cane sugar and coffee during winter in London, Chicago or Montreal is that of dependence. They come to require the maintenance of tropical conditions at home. That is, they come to rely and restrict themselves to over-heated surroundings. This nurtures an excessive dependence on fuel and central heating and ultimately reduces health and vitality.

A similar situation exists in tropical regions when temperate-zone diets rich in meat and heat-generating foods are eaten. In sunny Florida, southern California, Mexico, Spain and Israel, I have observed northern immigrants and visitors eat their regular "northern" diet and then experience considerable discomfort if their rooms and cars are not air-conditioned and their drinks aren't ice cold. I have found that with a traditional warm-region diet of fruits, salads, vegetable protein (e.g., beans) and less meat, much less artificial cooling is required.

When the demands for comfort exceed what would be sufficient to keep one's temperature regulated if regional and seasonal foods were eaten, then energy is being used inefficiently. Alienation and personal disorder often follow.

CHEMICAL FOOD

Eating imported and unseasonal foods has behavioral consequences. However, these are overshadowed by eating the *most alienating foods* of all—*those which are not a part of our natural environment.* That is, those foods that have been refined, processed, and chemically treated.

The use of chemical additives in food is widespread. In North America, there are over 3,000 food additives in use. How does this affect your daily bread? Well, there are over 40 chemical additives in some breads and the commercial baking industry in the United States uses 16 million pounds of chemicals a year.[3] Estimates vary. The average American consumes somewhere between six and ten pounds of chemicals each year.

The state of our daily bread reflects the alienation of our food. Today's "wholesome" loaf may contain as little as 50 percent wheat flour which has been stripped of much of its nutritional value. Mineral losses may be as follows:

Calcium	50% lost
Copper	60% lost
Iron	80% lost
Magnesium	70% lost
Potassium	50% lost
Zinc	70% lost

Vitamin losses are similar (page 77).

This deficient flour is then supplemented and treated with bleaching agents, mold retardants, dough conditioners, yeast, synthetic fats, artificial dyes, oxidizing agents, sugar and artificial sweeteners—all of which have been linked to allergic reactions and behavioral disturbances.

Artificial foods are being created to taste, look, and feel the way food should with the nutritional value food should have.

Today new food additives created by the powerful combination of imaginative chemistry and aggressive food technology have replaced Nature as the good fairy that helps fulfill (and create) our increasingly sophisticated food wishes. Do people desire strawberry-flavored creamy topping that can be frozen or refrigerated and that will not melt or wilt when placed on a pie months later? If so, it's thickening agents, artificial flavoring, preservatives, natural and artificial colorings and synthetic emulsifiers to the rescue.[4]

MICHAEL JACOBSON, *EATER'S DIGEST*

The problem is that people eating many of these foods may not be behaving as they should.

Some experts suggest that children are reacting unfavorably to the chemical additives in their food. Several scientists have reported that food coloring agents alone can lead to hyperactivity, learning disorders and allergic reactions in children.[5] These patterns may be characterized by uncontrollable outbursts of rage, the inability to concentrate and communicate, and depression. While the food-additive hypothesis has not always been substantiated in experiments, the feeling that artificial foods may have an adverse effect on behavior is definitely increasing.[6]

I discussed food and behavior with a leading Canadian psychiatrist and nutritionist who acknowledged that many unnatural foods were a cause of disordered and unnatural behavior. He repeated an expression which he attributed to a colleague, but which he himself considers something of a working principle, ''If it's man-made, don't eat it.''[7]

The field of clinical ecology has recently emerged. It attempts to define which chemical agents (in our food, water and air) can cause disorder and how, and to improve our relations with the technological world in which we live.[8] Well-controlled experimental research may ultimately define the relationship between specific additives and specific behavior disorders as well as what dosages produce effects.* However, some people are already convinced that many artificial foods and chemical additives are upsetting and generally hold the opinion that unnatural food leads to unnatural behavior.

SUPPLEMENTS GALORE

As people are eating more dis-integrated, extreme and alien foods they are becoming more and more reliant on food supplements to provide them with a nutritionally sound diet. The absence of certain nutrients can have a marked effect on behavior.

---

*There is currently speculation that low dosages of some food additives may be as harmful to health as high ones.[9]

The following table lists a host of psychological disorders that are thought to accompany a deficiency of four B vitamins.

DEFICIENCY OF	RESULTS IN
Thiamine (B_1) (found in whole grains, beans, nuts)	Depression, irritability, confusion, inability to concentrate, memory loss, appetite loss
Riboflavin (B_2) (found in whole grains, beans, greens, eggs)	Depression, fatigue
Niacin (B_3) (found in whole grains, beans, seeds, greens, meat)	Nervousness, irritability, apprehension, hallucination, confusion, insomnia
Cobalomin (B_{12}) (found in all naturally fermented foods e.g., sauerkraut, bran, pickles, yoghurt, miso, and some animal foods)	Agitation, depression, hallucination, difficulty in concentrating and remembering, paranoid behavior

Similarly, mineral deficiencies of calcium, copper, iron, magnesium, potassium, sodium and zinc have all been associated with abnormal physical and emotional states ranging from apathy, lethargy, and depression to hallucinations, irritability and emotional outbursts.[10]

From the data it is clear that nutrition can influence behavior directly. Normal psychological and physiological function depends on the presence of all nutrients in correct proportion. These can be found in a centered diet of natural foods. As I stated in Chapter 10, nutrient supplements are unnecessary for most people if they can *learn to eat* food that provides an adequate source of nourishment and not just eat whatever is available.

There is now evidence to suggest that the vitamins and minerals in food are reduced by:

- the tendency to pick and ship fruits and vegetables that are green rather than ripe

- soil depletion and the use of some chemical fertilizers (e.g., nitrates)
- food processing practices and freezing foods

as well as the consumption of refined foods, sugar, alcohol, chemical additives, birth-control pills, tobacco and drugs.

The solution is not simply taking vitamins, but eating wisely and well. That is, eating *natural,* wholesome food.* If you rely on getting your vitamins out of bottles rather than the food you eat, consider this:

- Vitamin supplements are unnatural and can have undesirable side effects (B_3, for example, often causes digestive upset, headache, irritability and undesirable skin reactions).
- According to chromatographic analysis, synthetic and chemically treated vitamins may be less effective than those occurring naturally in food.[11]
- Taking vitamins regularly undermines the body's natural capacity to manufacture them for itself.

People have an intuitive appreciation of food. They prepare it, eat it, enjoy it, discuss it and dream of it. On the contrary, there is no such intuition for vitamins, calories, proteins or minerals. People have repeatedly reported being overwhelmed or confused by lists of minimum daily requirements of nutrients. For example, what is your intuition or comprehension of the following advice offered by two respected researchers and psychodieticians who maintain ''supplements are necessary''? They suggest that a good one taken with each meal would supply these quantities of brain-cell nutrients per day.[12]

---

*By *natural* food I do not necessarily mean what is sold in health food stores—much of that food is highly processed and unnatural. Whole grains, fresh vegetables, fruits, nuts and healthy animal produce (preferably chemically untreated) are natural foods that can often be found in the marketplace.

Vitamin A	10,000–25,000	USP units
Vitamin B	1000–2500	USP units
Vitamin E	100–800	IU.
Vitamin C	300–1500	mg.
Vitamin B_1	10–25	mg.
Vitamin B_2	10–25	mg.
Vitamin B_6	10–25	mg.
Vitamin B_{12}	20–100	mg.
Bioflavanoids	50–200	mg.
Folic acid	75–100	mg.
Niacin	75–150	mg.
Pantothenic acid	50–200	mg.
PABA	25–50	mg.
Biotin	25–50	mg.
Choline	100–500	mg.
Imositol	100–500	mg.
Calcium	250–1000	mg.
Phosphorus	100–200	mg.
Iron	10–25	mg.
Copper	0.5–2	mg.
Iodine	0.15	mg.
Zinc	2–20	mg.
Manganese	2.20	mg.
Magnesium	20–300	mg.
Potassium	20–40	mg.

If you are attracted to the vitamin-mineral-supplement approach, buy a book listing all foods and their relative composition of vitamins, minerals, and protein.[13] Then if you have been told that you are lacking some nutrient, look it up and see which foods are rich in that nutrient. Try eating more of some that you enjoy and see how you feel. Time and again I have seen people buying bottles of supplements that they think they ought to have, but that they *don't really need* and furthermore don't understand.

Similarly, people sometimes try to correct imbalances by eating foods that they have been told provide certain nutrients, though these foods may not be appropriate or even desired.

One woman asked me about her husband, who had been told that he was "potassium deficient" and was therefore advised to eat six bananas a day—advice he apparently followed for some time.

I explained to her that *if* indeed her husband was deficient in potassium, then she and her husband could consult a book listing the mineral content of foods and select a number of those foods rich in potassium *that they enjoy*. (Such foods as beans, spinach, parsley, swiss chard, walnuts, peanuts, raisins, dates, figs, seaweeds and others contain significantly more potassium per weight than do bananas.) This seems a more reasonable approach than having her husband impose a monkey's share of bananas on himself each day.

> The most alienating foods of all are those which are not a part of our natural environment—chemical foods, chemical additives and chemically processed foods (including most food supplements).

The chemical additives best avoided are artificial flavors and colors and preservatives. Artificial flavors and colors fool the senses and upset the nervous system. Artificial preservatives (such as BHT, BHA, nitrates, nitrites, proprionates, benzoate and the sulphur compounds) alter the natural breakdown of food and also upset our biochemistry.

Nutrient supplements are extreme foods. They are either chemical synthetics or concentrates and derivatives of more centered natural foods. The latter may be appropriate following some cases of extreme depletion and/or imbalance. As a general rule, however, moving into the extremes is not the way to sanity and satisfaction; more frequently it leads to dependence, imbalance and perpetuates inappropriate eating habits and lifestyle. Whenever possible, it's preferable to eat wholesome, nutritious food (a centered, natural diet) than to rely on food supplements.

GROWING
OUR FOOD

The manner in which food is grown can affect behavior either directly or indirectly. Urbanization, specialization, and an increased demand for food have contributed to "farming" becoming more of a highly technological, mechanized and sometimes unnatural process.

There are some alternatives to present-day food production practices that are more economical and less alienating. One alternative that is being exercised is for people to play a greater role in growing their own food. Not only are homegrown foods usually fresher, better tasting and more economical, but contact with the earth is an integrating experience—a wonderful way to stay sane. Some psychiatric facilities and correctional institutions encourage their inmates to work in the garden in view of the therapeutic properties of working with plants and the earth.

On the Cork road in southern Ireland, I was given a ride by a diminutive, elderly farmer. As we traveled along he related the following bit of country wisdom:

> *If ye want a few hours of happiness, go out and get drunk.*
> *If ye want a few days of happiness, kill a pig,*
> *invite some friends and have a feast.*
> *If ye want a few weeks of happiness, then get yourself married.*
> *But, if it's a lifetime of happiness you're wanting, then sell the pig and grow*
> *a garden of food and flowers, and tend it a wee bit each day.*

For city dwellers this solution may not seem possible. However, along with backgarden plots and community allotments, an excellent source of fresh food (and vitamins) can be cultivated in microgardens in the home by sprouting a wide variety of seeds, grains and beans (e.g., alfalfa, sunflower, wheat, mung, and lentils).

ANIMAL FARM...
OR FACTORY

Animal farming methods can also affect behavior. Consider, for example, that a cow requires approximately 600 to 700 pounds of milk a year to feed a calf. Yet the typical dairy cow is selectively bred, fed and treated with chemicals and hormones to yield five to eight *thousand* pounds of milk annually. Chickens which once laid 30 eggs a year are now being stimulated into laying 300 eggs annually.

Similarly, meat for the table is artificially fattened with chemicals, supplements and growth stimulants (including sex hormones). Broiler chickens grow to two pounds in only six weeks, pigs reach 200 pounds in six months and steers may top 1,000 pounds in less than two years. In addition, these animals are routinely fed antibiotics and tranquilizers to further increase their weight and reduce the stress of their artificial lifestyle. The possibility that chemical residues and/or the deteriorated state of health of many of these animals may affect the consumer has been virtually ignored in spite of their obvious link to such problems as obesity, cancer and sexual disorders.

We may also consider the psychological state of these animals. In the process of being transported, penned and immediately prior to being slaughtered, animals experience a considerable amount of fear. A fascinating series of experiments on the chemical transference of learning suggests that psychological experience and predispositions to respond may be transmitted from one organism to another through the digestive process.

The general format of these experiments is that one group of animals (Group A) learns to perform a certain task to criterion while another group (Group B) does not experience the task. Both groups of animals are then killed and their brains and/or livers (presumably containing RNA and DNA) are fed or injected into two additional groups of animals. Group C receive the Group A ("experienced" animals); Group D receive B (naive animals). Studying a wide variety of animals (mammals, fish, and insects), investigators have found that Group C animals learned significantly more quickly, and with fewer errors than did Group D animals. The investigators conclude that the chemical transference of learning and experience between animals is possible.[14]

The implications of this research and the high production techniques of modern farming are quite thought-provoking, especially for those people eating large quantities of animal food.[15]

The consequences of eating foods created in factories and laboratories or from plants and animals which have been selectively bred, grown on chemicals and raised without an appreciation of the natural order have not been documented to the satisfaction of the scientifically minded. Regardless, some experts have suggested that on a cellular level, the effects may include disorders in which the cells come to grow or function out of harmony with the tissue surrounding them.[16]

Psychologically, people regularly eating chemically treated, artificial, and "stressed" foods may experience alienation, a lack of harmony with the natural order, and the dissatisfaction and unhappiness that engenders.

Fat foods are extreme foods.

Americans and Europeans eat too much fat—about 125 pounds of it a year per person in the U.S. Traditionally, fat constituted *less* than 30 percent of most peoples' diet. Today, for many people in the more affluent countries *over* 40 percent of their caloric intake is fat, much of which is eaten directly in high cholesterol foods.

Cholesterol is an essential chemical substance that our bodies can manufacture from the food we eat. On a low-cholesterol diet, the cholesterol ingested and manufactured by the body is used up in normal bodily function. On a high-cholesterol diet, the cholesterol ingested cannot be used up or eliminated and gets stored unwanted in spaces and places, including the blood vessels. If one continues to eat lots of high cholesterol foods, the storing process

Fat Foods, Milk Foods

Chapter **13**

continues, the blood vessels become occluded, the flow of blood, oxygen and nutrients to the brain and other organs decreases. Ultimately, this reduces health, performance and vitality.

The foods highest in cholesterol are *animal* foods, such as meat, eggs, cheese and butter. Their high incidence in the diet is unnatural and has been associated with a host of degenerative diseases, including:

- heart disease
- stroke
- vascular disease (including atherosclerosis, hardening of the arteries)
- diabetes
- cancer
- senility
- reduced sensory performance (e.g., deafness,* impaired vision).[1]

One answer to these problems is simply to *eat less fat,* and that doesn't mean just less animal fat (high cholesterol or saturated fat), but less vegetable fats and oils (unsaturated fats) as well.† Studies have shown that a low-fat *and* low-cholesterol diet will reduce degenerative disease more effectively than simply a low-cholesterol diet (which is often high in vegetable fats).[2] In practical terms this means that not only butter, but margarine and peanut butter should also be used sparingly.

A low-fat diet means low animal *and* low vegetable fat.

A "longevity center" in California treats a variety of degenerative disorders (primarily heart and vascular diseases) with a simple program of diet and exercise. The diet is centered and natural. It's no meat, no sugar, no salt, *and low fat* (no dairy foods, no peanut butter, no eggs, no salad or cooking oil). Essentially

---

*The fourth most used language in the United States is sign language.
†Least desirable are hydrogenated and saturated fats.

patients eat whole grains, vegetables, and fruit. The exercise program for most people involves walking...several miles each day.

The functional changes reported by those suffering from heart disease, atherosclerosis, high blood pressure and diabetes on this program have been extremely impressive. Favorable psychological changes have also been observed. Several patients have reported improved memory, greater clarity of thought (behaviors correlating with improved cerebral circulation), a more positive outlook and a marked reduction in anxiety. Many of those previously frightened by conditions of high blood pressure and heart disease report being able to live more normally without the fear of an impending stroke or heart attack.

Fatty foods are extreme foods...with extreme consequences. Fatty foods can have different effects on behavior. Some, such as eggs and meats, are very contractive foods and have a contractive effect. Others, such as milk, are less contractive and lead to a very different behavioral syndrome.

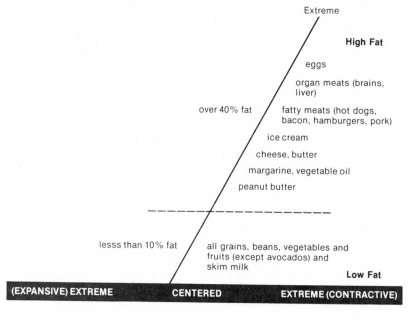

Dairy foods are milk, butter, cheese, yoghurt and cream.* Many people eat these foods because they believe them to be almost perfect, which they are not. If enjoyed, dairy food, like most things, can be used in moderation. However, when dairy foods become a major part of one's diet, or when used excessively, they can affect development and limit satisfaction.

"COW'S MILK IS FOR THE CALF"

Milk is the perfect food for the newborn. Mother's milk has all the nutrients in the correct proportion to support human development.

Most humans stop milk drinking and breast feeding when they begin to chew and can select foods for themselves. Weaning generally occurs somewhere between six months and two years of age.

Of all the mammals, only man—and then *only a minority of our species; principally the Caucasians—continues to eat milk and milk products past this age.* Indeed, some people are never really weaned. The average American adult consumes about 140 quarts of milk, 25 pints of ice cream and 16 pounds of cheese as part of the over 350 pounds of milk foods that they ingest annually.

Gandhi once said, "Cow's milk is for the calf." A baby calf may double its weight in the first six weeks of life (from 75 pounds to 150 pounds) and move about. To support this rapid growth, locomotor development, and the calf's great size and weight, an appropriate food substance has evolved—cow's milk.

---

*Skim milk and yoghurt are much less concentrated (contracted) than butter and cheese. Remember, there may be as much as 10 pounds of milk in one pound of cheese. In addition, yoghurt is somewhat predigested and more easily assimilated. Compared with ice cream, natural yoghurt contains less fat, fewer chemicals and is more digestible.

A human's needs are quite different. During the first six months, baby's development is focused more on the maturation of its nervous system than on an increase in bulk. (It may only gain a few pounds during this period.) A special substance has evolved to support this development. This substance is human milk. Whereas a child can be fed the milk of cows, goats, buffalos and mares, this is not in harmony with *natural* evolutionary patterns. For example, cow's milk and goat's milk have almost three times the amount of protein as does human milk, but only half the carbohydrate. Lots of protein may increase body size, but (natural) carbohydrate develops and feeds the nervous system.

There are several effects of substituting cow's milk for mother's milk in feeding children. Such feeding is undoubtedly a factor in the ever-increasing body size of humans, horizontally as well as vertically. Research findings suggest that the size and number of certain cells in the body are partially determined by the foods eaten in early life.[3] An excess of these cells predisposes the adult to obesity. This is consistent with a report that there is significantly more obesity in children who are bottle fed cow's milk than those who are breast fed mother's milk.[4]

Obviously, bigger is only better within limits. The marked increase in growth rate and body size in the past few generations correlates directly with the increased consumption of dairy food. Milk is the food that stimulates rapid expansion in the very young. However, too much cow's milk and its products can cause too much and too rapid expansion.

As a child, I was told that milk, butter and cheese were very healthful foods. Today, when these foods are being processed and consumed in excess, physicians are beginning to link dairy foods to a variety of physical ailments.[5] The list includes:

- *Allergic reactions*—cow's milk is one of the foods that children are most reactive to. Dairy foods can also sensitize the mucous membranes and thus increase reactivity to other seemingly unrelated substances (e.g., pollen and dust).

- *Atherosclerosis and some vascular diseases* (hardening of the arteries) are related to dairy and other high-fat foods. Atherosclerosis is present in most two-year-old American children.
- *Arthritis* has been linked to dairy food as well as other foods (meat and sugar) and circumstances.
- *Sinus problems and discharges, deposits, and blockages* in other parts of the respiratory system can be caused by excesses of dairy food.
- *Degenerative ailments,* including diabetes, heart disease, obesity, some intestinal disorders and cancers (e.g., breast cancer) may also be affected by dairy consumption.

In all cases, a marked reduction or elimination of dairy food is advised.

MILQUETOAST OR MILKSOP?

It is far more difficult to observe the psychological effects or personality changes that accompany eating large quantities of dairy food. One observer remarked:

> *Many of us watched the Red Cross handing glasses of milk to soldiers returning from the Asian theatre of World War II almost before they had come off the gangplank. The eagerness with which these men, long-deprived of family and familiar foods, took this glass of milk gave ample evidence of its meaning to them.... The soldier looks back to milk as in many ways expressing the comfort, security and contentedness of life as it was at home.* [6]

Many people find dairy foods comforting. Indeed, a warm milk drink before bed provides folks from 3 to 93 years of age security and comfort for a sound night's sleep. It's like being "tucked in."

A well-known Oriental teacher and philosopher has observed that cultures emphasizing dairy foods reflect a childlike perception and mythology. He noted that in the dairy-eating cultures of the West, religion was often based on a parent-child relationship to God. God is the Father and we are the children. He has also noted that in these dairy cultures there is often a childlike dependence which is expressed in terms of someone other than oneself (e.g., a messiah) who was or will be responsible for one's salvation.[7]

THE FOOD OF ATTACHMENT
(THE MOTHER-CHILD BOND)

Nursing is a time of very close attachment and dependence between mother and child. Through the intimacy and closeness of their bond the child receives physical and psychological nurturance. Physicians stress the importance of this period and breastfeeding in determining the immediate and long-term predisposition to disease.* Psychologists suggest that the rudiments of trust and social behavior are learned at the breast.

Mother's milk is the perfect food to nurture the infant in this critical period of psycho-physical development. Disrupting the natural feeding pattern by depriving an infant of nursing and substituting bottle feeding may have long-lasting psychological and physical consequences. It has long been thought that bottle feeding increases feelings of separation, fear and anxiety in the newborn with possible repercussions in later life.

---

*Breast-fed infants are more disease resistant than bottle-fed babies. It's reasonable to assume that differential dietary effects in adults may be confounded unless and until investigators take into account the early feeding experience of the individual and distinguish between those who were breast-fed and those who bottle fed.

As for prolonging milk drinking into adulthood, there hasn't been any psychological investigation to show that cow's milk leads to bovine behavior. Nor is there any psychological data to suggest that milk drinking (and dairy-food consumption) past infancy increases dependence, attachment and/or infantile behavior. However, in my personal life and practice I have observed that in *excess* dairy foods nurture and reinforce a tendency to behavior characterized by attachment, sentimentality, dependent thinking, and depression.*

Many people "hold" onto others and relationships in a way that restricts their growth and promotes dependence and depression.

One middle-aged lady who ate lots of dairy food contributed to her problems in just that way. She was a widow whose children had grown up and moved away. Her problem was that she made herself very unhappy due to her psychological need to have her children close by. Her "attachment" to them and not her love for them caused her unhappiness. When I later interviewed her two daughters (one married, both well past their teens), they explained that it was their mother's clinging, expectations and continuously "checking up" on them that made it difficult and unpleasant for them to live close by. "If only she could enjoy us without hanging on, we'd all be happier," said one of the daughters.

Like the Oriental philosopher, I have also observed that people eating lots of dairy food have a *tendency* to place responsibility for their behavior somewhere else. "I've been told that I can't..."; "I'm not allowed to..." or "supposed to..."; "My doctor said that I should...or shouldn't." They often delegate responsibility to a therapist, a wife, a teacher, a husband or a mother. This is in contrast with a more self-responsible attitude: "I've decided to try this," or "I'd rather not."

Habitual dairy eaters also tend to preface and color what they have to say with a good deal of sympathy and sentimental

---

*For quite different reasons, depression and dependent thinking can result from prolonged periods on a protein deficient or high sugar (and/or alcohol) diet.

behavior.* Compare the more sentimental "I'm so sorry for you"
..."Oh, you poor baby" (or thing), with the less emotional "I
see," or "I understand," to be followed by, "What do *you* plan to
do about it?"

These different reactions can have different effects on behavior.
Ancient Oriental philosophy taught that emotions interrelated
and that sympathy in the face of sorrow increases one's feelings of
self-pity, whereas confrontation and challenge reduce self-pity
and stimulate action.

IT'S UNNECESSARY
AND UNNATURAL

Most of mankind doesn't eat dairy food after weaning. Where it
has been eaten for centuries, it is generally consumed in propor-

---

*A note on *sentimental behavior:* Sentimentality has many connotations. I refer to sentimental
behavior as an excessively emotional reaction or attitude to a person or event.

Sentimental transactions are more characteristic of the parent-child bond than adult-adult
interactions.

In relation to diet, I have observed that lacto-vegetarians (dairy eaters) express more
sentimental behavior than non-lacto-vegetarians. For example, lacto-vegetarians often
express a sentimental explanation as the *primary* reason for their not eating meat—"It
causes suffering or cruelty to animals." (I might add that they say this unaware or in spite
of the fact that the dairy industry inflicts considerable suffering in animals. To maintain a
continuous high level of milk production, cows are repeatedly [and usually artificially]
impregnated, and their calves are taken from them shortly after birth—a painful process.)
In contrast, non-lacto-vegetarians usually cite reasons of health of "effects" as primary
with sentiment being less evident.

I've also observed different degrees of sentimentality amongst lacto- and non-lacto vegetarian spiritual groups in North America. In reference to teachers and gurus, lacto-
vegetarians (e.g., yogis) stress devotion (bhakti) and open displays of affection and sentiment. On birthdays, deathdays, celebrations and anniversaries, teachers, past gurus and
deities may be adorned with flowers, their pictures may be carried around on garlanded
floats and boats and pujas (milk baths of holy statues) may be performed in their honor. In
contrast, non-lacto-vegetarian groups (e.g., macrobiotics) tend to express far less sentiment and devotion to teachers and past associations. Similar differences in sentimental expression can be observed in relation to present associations and acquaintances.

tions less than in the West today and in a more chemically un-treated state. Today, dairy cows are given hormones, tranquilizers, antibiotics and penicillin. Their products are homogenized, ir-radiated, preserved, colored and supplemented with vitamins. As such, they can be very *un*natural foods.

Milk and milk products are unnecessary after weaning. Many people think they are a vital source of calcium.* They are unaware that there is as much calcium per weight in beet and mustard greens, watercress, sunflower seeds and almonds as in whole cow's milk; twice the calcium in sesame seeds and collard greens; and ten times the calcium in some seaweeds (hiziki, kelp).[8]

Some people seemed surprised to hear that my wife was *not* drinking milk or eating dairy food while she was breast feeding our son. "Don't you need calcium?" they asked. She sometimes reminded them that cows don't need to drink milk to make milk any more than chickens have to eat eggs to make eggs. While nursing she ate plenty of whole grains, green vegetables, sprouts, sesame seeds and whatever else she felt she wanted.

I used to eat lots of milk and cheese, but I stopped about ten years ago. Now, very occasionally, I enjoy some fresh butter, yoghurt or cheese. Once or twice a year, I may relish some cheese-cake, but usually a little is more than enough. Since I've stopped eating dairy foods regularly, the two most dramatic changes I have noticed in myself are:

1. I breathe easier. A recurrent sinus condition has disappeared.
2. I see things a little more clearly and a little less sentimentally.

---

*Human milk has one-third to one-half the calcium found in cow's and goat's milk, and that is ideal for human infants. Substituting cow's milk with its excessive protein and sodium for mother's milk is inappropriate, unbalancing and stressful to the infant. It specifically stresses the nervous system (which maintains a Na/K constant), the digestive system and the kidney.

WHAT YOU CAN PUT
ON YOUR TOAST

People ask what they can spread on their breakfast toast (hopefully, whole wheat!) in place of butter and cheese. One substitute that I occasionally use is sesame butter (*tahini*). This can be spread on toast and bread or mixed with other ingredients in making spreads, sauces and blended drinks. Another is an Oriental staple called *miso*. [9] Miso is a salty soybean paste (available in most natural food stores) which can be made into delicious spreads, sauces and soups. Still another is tofu, a soybean cheese not dissimilar to cottage cheese in its preparation and taste. [10] Tofu can also be enjoyable when added to a wide variety of dishes. Some people use soy milk or plant milk (though I don't). Like dairy food, tofu, soy milk, margarine,* sesame butter and all the nut butters are rich, *high-fat foods and should be used in moderation.*

If you enjoy dairy foods, I would advise that you eat them in moderation and that you select those that are chemically untreated. Milk, yoghurt, butter and cheese may contain preservatives, stabilizers and coloring agents, to name a few additives. Be conscious that, like all other foods, they have their effects—both physical and mental—some of which I have described in this chapter. One way of becoming more aware of these effects is to eliminate dairy foods from your diet for a two-week period. Instead, substitute lots of green vegetables, some sesame seeds, nuts, beans and even seaweed. See how you feel, think, and act. Then, reintroduce dairy foods into your diet and see if there is any change.

---

*Most margarines are rich in saturated fats and high in chemical additives. I rarely use them.

Quantity destroys quality... and sometimes beauty.

Overeating is another "unnatural" eating pattern with profound consequences to mental and physical well-being. Almost 1,000 years ago, it was written:

Overeating is like a deadly poison to any constitution and is the principal cause of all disease. Most maladies that affect mankind result from bad food or are due to the patient filling his stomach with an excess of food that may even have been wholesome. [1]

If you eat too much, your body just can't handle it efficiently. You become stressed, toxins accumulate, performance deteriorates and tension and disease result. The main effects of overeating are increased stress, disease and overweight.

Overeating and Obesity

Chapter **14**

It has been estimated that there are between 40 and 80 *million* obese or extremely fat people in the United States alone.[2] That's at least one person in five. Since obesity is so common and so obvious, it follows that overweight is the dietary problem that has received most psychological study.

For some time, psychologists have been aware that eating behavior is regulated by both internal and external cues. Internal cues refer to stimuli from within our bodies such as stomach contractions and blood-sugar level. External cues include such factors as how the food appears, how it tastes and the time of day it is consumed. Most of us make use of both sets of cues. Fat people, however, seem to rely less on internal and more on external factors to tell themselves when to eat. For example, fat people will eat as much on a full stomach as they would on an empty stomach... and they are more apt to eat quickly and not chew thoroughly. Fat people will also eat more of something when they think it is the right time to eat. In one experiment, the clocks in the laboratory were secretly advanced to make it appear much later than it actually was and much closer to dinner time.[3] Under these conditions, obese subjects presumably thinking it was dinner time and that they therefore must be hungry, ate significantly more than did normals.

WHY PEOPLE ARE OBESE

Various explanations have been advanced to account for why obese people make less of internal cues than do normals. This phenomenon has been related to faulty brain control (specifically, lesions of the ventromedial and lateral hypothalamus). Others have suggested that it may be a function of child-rearing practices.

One such theory was that fat people mislabel hunger because of the way they were handled and fed as infants. If mother fed the infant in response to any discomfort, the individual might ultimately mislabel all unpleasant internal states as hunger, or might eat whenever upset.[4] Alternatively, if a child was rewarded with food for behavior, he or she might later think eating was a way of rewarding or being good to oneself. Then there is the common practice discussed earlier of feeding babies "unnatural" foods such as sugar and cow's milk in large quantities. Not only might the former distort taste, but both may lead to a surplus of fat cells which may mean a lifetime's legacy or predisposition to being fat.

Constitutional differences may explain why some people can eat certain foods and not gain weight and others can't. Body type, intestinal length, and astrological make-up have all been linked to appetite and overweight. It is rarely these differences that are the cause of obesity.

It is generally agreed that most obesities can be attributed to an excess of food intake beyond the demands of normal energy expenditure. That is to say, fat people eat too much. One investigator reported that 96 percent of the obese people he studied showed some metabolic disturbance. He considers this dysfunction to be the *result*, and not the cause, of eating an inappropriate diet for a prolonged period of time.[5] Indeed, the early notion that people eat too much because of some deep-seated glandular imbalance no longer seems to be popular.

While metabolic differences may not account for obesity, they may explain why some foods affect people differently. One psychochemist looked specifically at the rate at which people burn up or oxidize their food and found some marked differences.[6] On the basis of his findings he split people into two groups—the slow oxidizers and the fast oxidizers. Slow oxidizers burn up their food slowly and hence should avoid eating foods that burn up slowly. Such foods may lead to an increase in weight as well as biochemical and behavioral upset. Fast oxidizers burn up their foods quickly and are advised to avoid foods that burn up quickly. A list of some of the foods that he suggests be *used sparingly* by both types are shown in the table below:

Fast Oxidizers	Slow Oxidizers
Candies, pastries, fruit juice, jellies, ice cream, potatoes, white rice, spaghetti, crackers, lettuce, green peppers, raw onions, cabbage, pickles, milk, buttermilk, cottage cheese, catsup, spicy sauces, soft drinks, coffee, tea, beer and wine	Pastries high in fat and low in flour (e.g., cheesecake), avocados, beans, peas, cauliflower, spinach, asparagus, liver, kidney, caviar, lard, butter and hard alcohol

This research on oxidation rate suggests that people with differing metabolic rates may perform and feel best if they avoid certain foods, principally extreme and refined foods. Oxidation rate, however, is not fixed. Although it is affected by genetics and early feeding patterns, it is also influenced by present eating habits, which can be changed.

I have observed that after an extended period on a centered diet, people often change their preferences away from the extremes and become more centered. A centered diet may be a more appropriate long-term therapy and way of life than simply restricting oneself to food in one extreme. Furthermore, the food lists given include many foods that are inappropriate to man. All "sweets," refined carbohydrates, soft drinks, ice cream, spices, coffee and alcohol are not healthful foods, particularly for people with mental and physical problems. The consumption of all such foods should be reduced not by just one type of person. They should be used sparingly by everyone.

FATMAN'S FANCY

There has been little psychological research on the behavioral effects of many of the foods prescribed for weight reduction. Most calorie counters seem to feel that carbohydrates are taboo and that they should avoid them *all*. They lump together as carbohydrates whole grains and refined carbohydrates such as cookies and sugar. While the latter may make you fat, whole grains will not, nor will reasonable quantities of farm-fresh corn or garden-fresh peas, which are often considered fattening.

> What's fattening is immoderate eating habits—eating too much, eating extreme foods, sweets and desserts, concentrated foods, fat foods and unnatural food.

The blanket avoidance of all carbohydrates by weight-conscious people in order to eliminate the refined carbohydrates (especially sugar and white flour) from their diet deprives them of their principal food and forces them to eat in the extremes. The popular "get slim, high-protein diet" with low or no carbohydrate is both unbalancing and unsatisfying. It may provide a short-term means of shedding weight but it inevitably leads to strong cravings (meat attracts sweet) and bingeing frequently follows.

Meat is concentrated (contractive) energy. Most of the meat eaten is from animals who have been treated with chemical additives, supplements and hormones *to increase their weight*. Eating sizable quantities of meat containing residues of these fattening substances can lead to weight increases in the consumer.

> The formula for weight loss and weight control is quite straightforward. Eat a centered diet, avoid extreme and unnatural foods, chew your food well, exercise and don't overeat.

On a friend's farm in southern Spain, I was introduced to an engaging and very obese woman. In conversation it was mentioned that I was writing a book on food and psychology. The lady remarked that she was very interested in the subject. In fact, she was the head of a diet-watching organization in the midwestern United States. She explained that for some time she had managed to control her weight, and then she went on a binge and her present obesity was the result. As we talked, it became clear that she did not distinguish between whole and refined carbohydrates (remember, it's the latter that puts on weight). Nor did she appreciate balance; that meat attracts sweet. In short, her appreciation of food and its effects was limited. She had tried to control her problem rather than learn how to make balance and live. Over a dinner of brown rice, lentils, greens and a large salad, I explained that if she ate *slowly* and *chewed* her food well she could eat as much of these foods as she wanted and she wouldn't gain weight appreciably. It was welcome news, for she appeared happy, and, despite her overweight state, said, "That's great; let's eat, I'm famished!"

Following a lecture in California, I was greeted by a middle-aged business man who was friendly, overweight and diabetic. "I enjoyed what you had to say," he remarked. "I love to eat grains and beans, but I've been told that I shouldn't with my weight and diabetic problems." Further inquiry revealed that for years he had been eating lots of dairy food instead. I reminded him that just as too much sugar turns to fat, the converse also applies; too much fat (dairy) upsets blood-sugar level and puts on weight. Experts now recognize that both sweets and fats can increase the triglycerides, serum lipids and cholesterol in the blood and that high levels of these compounds correlate with obesity, diabetes and vascular disease. With a little encouragement he decided he was going to reduce his consumption of dairy foods and start eating more whole grains and beans. "It's what I've been missing for a long time," he said.

Still another obese gentleman was disturbed by the government's ban on artificial sweeteners. He complained that if he couldn't use saccharin then he'd have to use sugar and he would get even fatter. I explained to him that his habit of eating too much meat was one reason for his excessive sweet tooth (and his excessive weight). I suggested that he adopt a more centered diet rather than eating and balancing in the extremes.

When I was younger I had an insatiable sweet tooth and I sometimes ate too much. As I stated earlier, I solved the first problem by eating far less extreme foods. My tendency to eat too much remains, though it has lessened a good deal from my teens when I could make stacks of pancakes or quarts of milk disappear. I still eat more than is necessary for optimal health and sensitivity. However, I have made two observations since adopting a centered diet of natural food:

1. I have a greater and more lasting sense of satisfaction and lightness than I did on a diet of extreme foods.
2. I can eat what I want and I don't gain weight.

LOSING WEIGHT

With one in every five Americans overweight, two predictions might be made: (1) there are many methods suggested for treating obesity, and (2) most of them are not very effective. A few of the more popular approaches are:

1. *Medication:* Stimulant drugs (usually sympatho-mimetic amines) are prescribed to suppress appetite. They work by stimulating the sympathetic nervous system which reduces the activity of the digestive system. While these drugs do suppress appetite, they are very extreme and can be quite imbalancing. They may also have behavioral side effects such as nervousness, agitation and exhaustion. They are the fat man's "speed" and speeding can be dangerous.[7]

2. *Dieting:* Many reducing diets are advised. Some such as mono or duo diets recommend eating just one or two foods (e.g., grapes or grapefruit and eggs) for several weeks. On "filler" diets, people fill up for ten days or two weeks on low-calorie chemical preparations. The high-protein diets discussed earlier are probably the most popular of all the reducing diets. One expert summarized the impact of these diets as follows: "All studies of the long-range effectiveness of dieting show that within a year 90% of individuals who lose weight gain it

back."[8] Another popular method is the calorie counting or waistline-watching approach. This approach usually provides some lists of foods to be avoided (fattening) and to be eaten (non-fattening) and rules for how frequently to eat each day and the times that meals and snacks should be eaten. Many people prefer to be told what and when to eat and what and when not to eat. This method may be an effective aid for some of them. However, it is usually uncentering and restrictive.

3. *Fasting or therapeutic starvation:* If you don't eat, then you'll obviously lose weight. Like the high-protein diet, though, this is an extreme and contractive process—one that is frequently followed by bingeing and overeating (extreme contraction leads to extreme expansion). Furthermore, it doesn't teach people what and how to eat each day. Fasting a day or two a month or a few days every few months is fine if you enjoy it; however, long-term fasting should be supervised.

4. *Surgical techniques.*

5. *Acupuncture:* This technique is now being used to treat obesity. Some acupuncturists report favorable results, some don't.[9] Generally, the points stimulated relate to the hypothalamus (the eating center of the brain), the sympathetic nervous system or the stomach and intestines. Treatment is directed at reducing appetite. Sound dietary advice may or may not be given.

6. *Hypnosis:* Hypnosis has been used to help people overcome (various) insatiable appetites for many years. It is frequently administered without any sound dietary advice. The long-term results have not been impressive.

7. *Psychotherapy:* This technique is helpful in uncovering many of the psychological reasons as to why people overeat and being fat almost always intensifies or increases one's psychological problems. Psychotherapy can help to change self-awareness, self-image and attitudes. It is *not* the most effective approach to weight control. It can be a lengthy and costly

process and may not provide any advice about what and how to eat. In cases of obesity, psychological counseling should be combined with dietary counseling.

8. *Behavioral techniques:* Behavioral techniques are increasingly being used for weight control. This includes a broad range of techniques from aversive conditioning to training in self-regulating food intake. In aversive conditioning, states of discomfort such as electric shock and vomit-inducing drugs are presented to the overweight person prior to his or her eating or visualizing certain forbidden, fattening "target" foods. In theory, an associative link forms between these foods and the unpleasant stimuli and the foods lose their attractiveness.

Some years ago, I worked as a psychologist in Canada's first behavior therapy unit where we experimented with this approach for weight loss and alcoholism. My impressions then, and studies since, suggest that aversive methods rarely lead to lasting behavioral change, possibly because sooner or later exposure to the food occurs in the absence of the unpleasant stimulus. Moreover, the goal, as I see it, is to increase one's awareness and pleasure in eating, not to make the experience unpleasant and unnatural.

The self-regulation training approach has proven somewhat more effective in dealing with weight control. It focuses on training people how to control many of the external cues and factors that influence and determine how they eat. Some of the factors relate to the attractiveness of the food, eating speed, eating frequency and general eating awareness.

While studies using the self-regulation training approach report "statistically significant" results, the actual magnitude of the weight loss has not been impressive. In a review of over 100 reported studies of weight control involving people between 50 to 100 pounds overweight, *less* than a quarter of the studies reported losses of more than 20 pounds. The follow-up data are equally unimpressive and the dropout rate for subjects was almost 50 percent.[10]

In a more recent review of the behavioral treatment of obesity it was reported that the average weight loss for a group of 125 men and women averaging over 215 pounds was only 11 pounds.[11] These findings are consistent with 21 other studies which showed an average weight loss of 11.5 pounds in 458 obese individuals. While the magnitude of this weight loss (approximately 11 pounds) is statistically significant, it is not particularly impressive when one considers the extreme overweight condition of most of the subjects in this research.

There is no doubt that overweight people frequently have poor eating habits and that attempting to regulate external cues and instruct them *how* to eat can be very helpful in improving their eating behavior. The limited long-term effectiveness of such procedures comes from a consideration of behavior without an appreciation of the content and balance of food. You can't talk meaningfully about *how* to eat without understanding something about *what* to eat.

How to eat—like *what* we eat—has a profound effect on our behavior. In effect they go together—one is form, the other is content. If you are overweight, then you'll likely appreciate and benefit from a little guidance in modifying your eating habits. Five recommendations for people seeking information on how to eat are:

- Take a warm drink 15 to 20 minutes before each meal.
- Relax.
- Eat slowly.
- Increase your eating awareness.
- Eat when you feel hungry.

These recommendations apply to almost everyone, fat and thin alike.

How to Eat

Chapter **15**

Take a Warm Drink 15 to 20 Minutes Before Each Meal. I suggest
that a warm drink—soup, broth, even warm water (but preferably
neither coffee nor anything sweet)—15 to 20 minutes before a
meal helps to reduce the amount eaten and the speed of eating.
Obese people are more sensitive to the caloric value of *liquid* rather
than solid food.[1] Fifteen to 20 minutes is sufficient time for the
satiety mechanism to be activated. It also makes it less likely that
your plate will be cleaned before you are aware of it and while you
still feel empty.

This technique is helpful and by no means unique. Throughout Europe and Asia, people take soup, tea or a warm drink prior
to eating. This is also in keeping with the "natural meal." Scientists measuring the flow of mother's milk have noted that during
the first few minutes, the milk is a thin liquid. As the baby starts
to quench its thirst and begins to fill up, a thicker, more nutritious
milk begins to flow. This natural control for overeating of fluid
first and nutrient second can be incorporated into a practice that
helps you to control overeating.

Relax. Prior to any meal, take a few minutes to collect yourself,
to allow your tensions to leave you, to be silent, to listen. You can
consider this relaxation, meditation or prayer. Try to avoid ap-
proaching your food with haste, tension or anger. All three states
stimulate the sympathetic nervous system and inhibit digestion.

Eat Slowly. Sit down, be comfortable, take your time and *chew
your food well.* To start with, plan enough time to eat leisurely. At
the beginning of a meal, say to yourself, "I'm going to take 45
minutes (or an hour) for this meal." Once determined, use the
full time. Time taken for a meal increases your eating enjoyment.
It also improves your digestion and enables you to be happier and
more efficient the rest of the day. Avoid eating on the run or grab-
bing a bite. If you are that rushed, skip the meal or just have a
warm drink.

Another helpful hint is to slow the pace of your eating by
taking a one-minute break from eating every five minutes through-

out the meal. Simply put down the fork or spoon and relax. Actually, putting down the fork or spoon between mouthfuls can also help cut down eating too fast or too much, though it's a practice people don't seem to stick to. It is also very important, for a number of reasons (Chapter 10), to chew your food well—20 to 50 times per mouthful. If counting reminds you to chew, then by all means count the number of times you chew until chewing well becomes an established habit. Lastly, I find that sitting back in my chair with both my feet on the ground and remembering to allow myself to *breathe naturally* helps me to slow down when I'm eating too fast and thus helps me not to overeat.

Increase Your Eating Awareness. An interesting experiment, and one that heightens awareness, is to write down everything that you eat during a two-week period along with the time of day it was eaten. Many people have reported being surprised (and even embarrassed) to discover just how much they ate or patterns to their eating (such as bedtime or between meal snacks) that they were unaware of.

Freeing eating from competitive activities also helps to increase eating awareness. The dinner table is not the place to read, watch TV or get involved in an emotionally-charged conversation. Nor is a stony silence required. Try to structure an eating situation that allows or even encourages you to be aware of what you are eating; the speed of your eating; your chewing; your breathing; the delicious taste of the food; and the pleasure of eating. This kind of awareness requires some active attention on your part.

Eat When You Feel Hungry. Some experts advise people to eat three meals and two snacks a day; others advise two meals and no snacks. I generally advise people to eat when they feel hungry and to remember to be aware of what and how they eat. I also advise them to eat natural whole foods (not convenience or "junk" food), to take their time and to chew their food well.

Most experts suggest that the largest meal be at the middle of the day. Like everything else, this varies with who you are, where you live and what you do. Many overweight people seem to do well if they just have a light breakfast, perhaps just a warm drink, and do not eat a meal until lunch. However, if they wake up one morning and feel really hungry, then I would suggest that they have something to eat. I wouldn't advise people to be rigid about anything, especially about when to eat their big meal. The one point on which almost all experts agree is *don't eat immediately before going to bed.* Not only will that disturb your sleep, but it will put on weight.

Following a lecture on food and behavior, I was approached by a young professional woman. She said: "I quite agree that I should take time in eating, that I should eat a centered diet and avoid snacking on junk food. However, sometimes I come home from work and I'm famished. Without really being aware of what I'm doing I've opened the fridge and devoured the first thing I can get my hands on. What do you advise me to do?"

I explained to her that not eating is contractive. When people are very hungry, they often want instant fullness or instant expansion. What would be appropriate is something expansive that fills them up easily and that doesn't require much chewing. When people are very hungry, they forget to chew. Liquid, preferably warm liquid (a cup of broth or an herbal tea), would be fine. Next best might be a fruit or a stick of raw celery.

I suggested that a cup of herbal tea, a glass of fruit juice, a stick of celery, or a fruit might remove the edge from her hunger and afford her sufficient time and composure to prepare something more substantial for her meal. It would also enable her to eat slowly with awareness and enjoyment.

Learning how to eat can be freeing, but set rules, such as eating only at prearranged times or a specified number of times a day, avoiding favorite foods (even if wholesome), keeping food locked away between meals and limiting the quantity of your meal are not freeing practices.

In my experience, the most satisfying and freeing practice (for fat and thin alike) is to eat a centered, natural diet—to eat slowly, with awareness, and when hungry. Eating this way you can gradually learn to follow your natural tastes and needs, adding a bit of this or less of that as required or desired.

Many people seem to feel that their chaotic eating habits—particularly overeating—are due to a lack of satisfaction in some other area. In helping them with their problems I have often found it helpful to advise them what and how to eat. Just as our emotional state and satisfaction can affect how and what to eat, how and what we eat can affect our emotional state and satisfaction.

One obese young man attributed his overeating to the considerable frustration and stress he experienced in his business and his personal life. "Some people drink when they get uptight; some take drugs," he explained. "I eat."

I acknowledged that frustration can contribute to overeating, but it is not a behavior that helps one to cope with their problems. Rather, overeating and excessive weight usually create far more problems than they solve. Learning how and what to eat predisposes you to relate to yourself and your responsibilities most effectively.

A NOTE ON INDIGESTION

Indigestion is a catch phrase for a variety of symptoms which seem to follow inappropriate eating behavior. The symptoms include gas, heartburn, pain, mucous, heaviness, distention and general discomfort. They may be accompanied by such behaviors as irritability, impatience, nervousness, fatigue, insomnia and depression.

The primary causes of indigestion are:

1. *Eating too much:* One simply cannot properly process excessive quantities of food.
2. *Eating too much extreme food:* Excesses of contractive foods (meat, fish, eggs) and fatty foods slow transit times and inhibit di-

gestion. Expansive foods (sugar, coffee and alcohol) create hyperacidity which upsets both the digestive tract and the digestive process.

3. *Eating too late:* Eating too close to bedtime is another reliable cause of indigestion. Healthy digestion requires time and activity. Eating before bedtime (especially the more dense, contracted, acid-forming foods, like meat) is apt to make sleep less restful and may contribute to disturbing dreams. (Specific foods may influence dreams in specific ways.)

4. *Eating too quickly:* Eating too fast and not chewing food properly, especially those foods like cereal grains which are partially digested in the mouth, causes acidity and indigestion. Again, even wholesome, well-balanced food will not be properly digested if eaten "on the run."

5. *Eating when emotionally upset:* When you are tense, angry or frightened, your sympathetic nervous system is activated. This fight or flight mechanism directs blood and energy to the periphery of the body, thus inhibiting digestion. In contrast, when you are relaxed, your parasympathetic nervous system which controls digestion is dominant and the digestive process is facilitated.

6. *Eating foods that do not combine well together:* Poor combinations of food inhibit digestion (see page 35). Too many different foods, especially those which are processed at different rates in different parts of the digestive system, are best not combined.

In this section, three psychological problem areas currently attracting considerable interest are discussed in terms of their relationship to food. These areas are: sexual disorders; educational disorders in children; and food-induced emotional responses (cerebral food allergies).

THREE
SPECIFIC PROBLEMS

Section **IV**

Sexual satisfaction, like satisfaction in life, involves balancing the expansive and contractive forces in nature.

Some psychologists and psychiatrists maintain that sexual problems underlie all neurotic behavior. While not all support this hypothesis, most would at least agree that sexual dysfunction accompanies mental and physical disorder. Since there is a popular concern with sexual performance, and since diet has a marked effect on behavior, it is not surprising that people have sought an aid to the former in the latter.

Scientific research on the relation of food and sex has been limited, but over the ages there has been a good deal of popular interest in identifying those foods that intensify sexual motivation, performance and pleasure—the aphrodisiacs.

Sexual Disorders

Chapter **16**

An appreciation that certain foods are sexually stimulating was evident in biblical times. For example, Rachel said to Leah, "Give I pray thee of thy son's mandrakes ... therefore he shall lie with thee tonight." (Genesis 30:14). Along with mandrake and its plant relatives, the tomato and the potato, other foods reported to be aphrodisiacs include: asparagus, avocado, beans, bird's nest soup, buckwheat, celery, hard cheeses (e.g., Gorgonzola, Parmesan), cocoa, eggs (especially raw), fish (particulary shellfish, oysters, mussels, fish eggs, fish oil, and shark fin soup), honey, lecithin, lettuce, most meats, olives, olive oil, most seeds (including cereal grains), all root plants (carrots, burdock and especially ginseng), the onion family (garlic, onions, leeks and scallions) and sesame. Many spices and herbs are said to possess sexually stimulating properties. These include: cloves, licorice, mustard, nutmeg, pepper, peppermint, thyme and golden seal.[1]

The effect of any food or herbal preparation depends on the recipient's state of sensitivity and reactivity. Sensitivity and reactivity are a function of constitution, lifestyle and daily diet. Some of the foods above may indeed sexually stimulate some people. Some affect me in that way.* What affects your neighbor, though, may not affect you. For example, the Spanish, a meat-eating people, were relatively insensitive to the herbal medicine of the corn-eating Incas. Unaffected by these preparations, the Europeans assumed them to be a collection of superstitious remedies —which some may have been. However, the Indians had a sophisticated appreciation of herbs as they related to their own chemistry. Similarly, the Great Lakes Indians were said to use 130 species of plants for food and over twice that number for medicinal purposes.[2] Yet, few of their remedies are used in current medical practice.

---

*As for those foods that *are* sexually stimulating, they rarely promote satisfying sexual relations. Eating to increase sexual satisfaction generally means eating to be more natural and balanced and not overeating sexually stimulating foods.

Sexual disorders are not isolated phenomena. The same syndromes of disintegration, alienation, insensitivity and extreme behavior that are expressed in other aspects of human activity also occur in sexual behavior.

There are, of course, social factors that contribute to and intensify sexual disorders. For example, in the course of "growing up," children are often conditioned not to express themselves in certain "sexual" ways. Often, natural actions involving the sexual organs are considered disgusting or rude and not to be seen by others. The result is that some people repress or deny their sexual feelings and desires. Others may experience guilt and embarrassment about normal (healthy) behavior.

Sexual dissatisfaction has many causes, but it can be related to and exacerbated by the food we eat. Basically, three dietary patterns nurture sexual dissatisfaction. They are:

1. an extreme diet
2. unpolarized eating
3. eating too much and too rich.

An Extreme Diet: Strong Urges and Strange Ideas. In general, contractive foods stimulate the lower energy centers (chakras) and expansive foods stimulate the higher centers. The more contractive the food, the more intense is the need to discharge. That is not to say, of course, that a strong need for sexual discharge leads to healthy and pleasurable sexual relations. In fact, it usually does *not.*

Generally, extreme foods, rather than intensifying sexual satisfaction, will reduce it. Extreme contractive (and high cholesterol) foods such as organ meats, eggs, hard cheeses, fish and

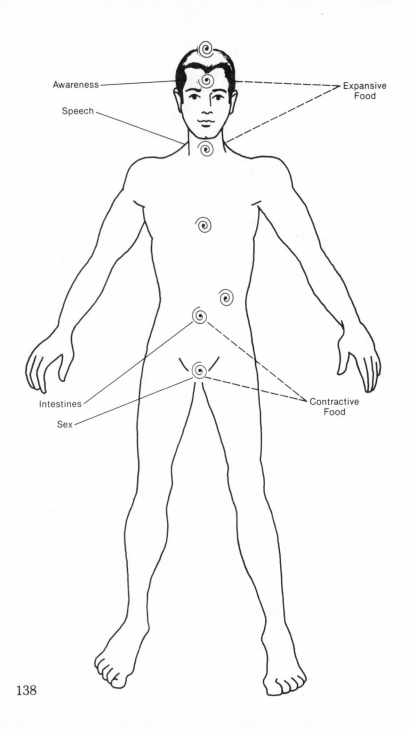

shellfish have been universally described as sexual stimulators. However, for most people who eat large quantities of these foods *regularly,* they have no noticeable effect.

According to an ancient maxim, anything in the extreme turns into its opposite. It appears that an excess of extreme contractive foods is apt to *decrease* sexual sensitivity and satisfaction.

Extreme expansive foods, such as sweets and sugar, also contribute to sexual difficulties. At one level, they lead to blood-sugar disorders, hypoglycemia and emotional upset as well as impotence and premature ejaculation.* They also stimulate vague and unrealistic thoughts and expectations which do not facilitate social and sexual communication.

> The average American, eating 240 pounds of meat and 120 pounds of sugar each year, may have strong urges and strange ideas regarding sex. That is, this extreme diet may stimulate a desire for sexual discharge and at the same time promote unrealistic sexual attitudes and expectations. Combined, these two factors nurture a widespread preoccupation with sex, private and public sex fantasies, perversions, the growing problem of incest and crimes of sexual violence.

In my personal life, and in my practice, I have found that a centered diet of whole grains with suitable additions of contractive foods (root vegetables, seeds, beans and some animal food) and balanced portions of expansive foods (leafy greens and some fruits) will, over time, lead to more integrated and satisfying (sexual) functioning.

Unpolarized Eating. Vive la différence! Men, relative to women, are constitutionally or innately more expansive. This is evidenced by their larger physical structure and the location of their sex organs on the surface of their body. Women are more contractive. Their structure is smaller and their sexual organs are within.

---

*Unstable blood-sugar levels (hypoglycemia and disglycemia) correlate with lower sex hormone (testosterone) production in males and sexual dysfunction.

To balance these innate tendencies, man is attracted to slightly more contractive stimuli, including food such as meat and fish. In contrast, woman is attracted to slightly more expansive stimuli, including foods such as sweets and fruits.

Diet was one factor in maintaining sexual polarity in traditional Japanese culture. I am told that women did not eat much contractive animal food—only small quantities of fish, and then only at appropriate times (such as in cold weather). Too much fish was thought to have a masculinizing influence leading to more aggressive behavior and changes in secondary sex characteristics (such as facial hair and hairy legs). Men, it was said, should not eat expansive foods such as fruits and sweets, for these would reduce their masculinity.

This idea was not confined to Japan. Herodotus quoted Cyrus, the Persian king, as saying, "Soft countries give birth to soft men. There is no region which produced delightful fruit and at the same time a warlike spirit."[3]

If all this sounds a bit foreign, remember that a similar appreciation is evident in America today when a man displaying non-masculine behavior may be referred to as "a fruit." Females are frequently referred to as fruits, sweets or other expansive foods when their femininity is being acknowledged... "She's a peach, tomato, sugar, honey." Similarly, motivational researchers in America have reported that, "In our studies, we found fascinating contrasts in the sexual attributes of food. The two extremes are meat and cake; the latter being the most feminine of foods."[4]

Today, men are eating lots of sweets and fruits; women are eating lots of meat and eggs...and sexual polarity is decreasing. If an individual is experiencing decreased sexuality and wants to do something about it, an alteration in diet could help to reverse this tendency. Alterations include the marked reduction of extreme and alienating foods. In the case of men, fewer expansive foods should be eaten, among them sweets, fruits, honey, wine and expansive dairy foods such as milk and ice cream. Females should reduce their intake of highly contractive foods such as meat, eggs and fish. In both cases, a marked reduction of all excessively con-tractive or expansive food is advised along with the adoption of *a centered diet*. It is rarely advisable to adopt the opposite extreme in diet for any extreme is apt to be taxing, unbalancing and lead to behavior that is unsatisfying.

Hormones. Diet may influence sexuality in another more complex manner. The word "hormone" comes from a Greek word (horman) meaning "to urge on." Animals secrete hormones which stimulate specific organs and urge them to function in certain species specific ways. Hormones also influence human functions.

Sexual hormones have a marked effect on human sexual appearance and behavior. Animal and synthetic hormones are used in the treatment of a wide variety of sexual disorders as well as sex-unrelated problems. They do, however, have side effects.*
For example, mothers given DES (diethyl stilbestrol) gave birth to female offspring with an increased incidence of vaginal cancer and male children with an increased incidence of urogenital anom-alies and homosexuality.[5] What makes this finding relevant to the discussion of diet and sexuality is that until recently DES was regularly fed to livestock (from beef to chickens) to increase their growth and size. DES and similar substances are then transmitted to the meat-eating consumer in the flesh they eat.

No well-controlled studies have shown the effects of DES residues in meat on human sexual behavior. It has been reported, however, that animals fed DES-treated meat became sterile. In humans, DES residues have been linked to breast cancer and menstrual disorders in women, impotence and sterility in men, and both accelerated maturation and arrested development in children.[6]

The use of steroid hormones in feeding cattle is still common practice. They are used primarily to promote increases in growth

---

*An increased incidence of cancer, tumors and cysts was observed in animals treated with DES.

rate and size. They also have an effect on the sexual behavior of animals. Specifically, they suppress the estrus cycle ("heat"), making the animal more docile and manageable.

Broiler and laying chickens are similarly fed hormones that alter their reproductive cycles.

The effect of all such compounds on the sexual behavior and appearance (including weight) of the consumer have been relatively ignored.

Eating Too Much and Too Rich. Eating too much, especially too much rich and fatty food, may also suppress sexual drive. Indeed, it is often a substitute for sex. An excess of rich and fatty foods has the effect of reducing energy flow and sensitivity. A reduction in sensitivity and blocked energy is a factor attracting many people to unusual and often unnatural means of sexual stimulation and gratification.

One woman I saw had a sexual problem. She had been expertly advised to follow an elaborate procedure of self-stimulation (and mechanical stimulation) to help her prepare herself to achieve more complete and satisfying sexual relations. This advice was given *independently* of the fact that she ate too much; especially too much food rich in animal fat. After some counseling and with appropriate changes in her diet (to a more centered, less rich fare) she reported greater satisfaction in her social and sexual relations.

A final note on the inter-relationship between diet and sexual behavior. Many of those interested in this subject would like to improve their sexual behavior—to have their performance match their ideas and fantasies. For most people, however, a healthy sexual adjustment is not simply a change in sexual performance, but a change in their sexual attitudes as well. Indeed, increased satisfaction is as apt to come from sublimating and redirecting sexual energy as from heightening sensitivity and experiencing a more total orgasm.

Sex therapy, sex counseling and sex clinics are becoming increasingly available to the public. These facilities have undoubtedly provided many individuals with beneficial re-education and guidance. Rarely is diet counseling included. A centered, natural diet would increase the effectiveness of any program aimed at heightening sexual and personal satisfaction.

Junk food is the food of the learning-problem generation.

Psychologists, educators and parents are becoming increasingly aware of children with educational problems. According to some recent estimates, educational problems affect up to one-third of all school children in the United States.

The child with an educational problem is one who is not performing up to a certain acceptable standard in the classroom. It may be that the child has a specific learning disorder and has trouble acquiring reading, speech or mathematical skills. It may be that the child has a disciplinary problem and is upsetting teacher, classmates or procedure. It may also be that the child has an emotional or physical problem which is decreasing its learning ability and/or making it difficult to behave in an acceptable manner. Any or all of these problems may constitute an educational problem.

Educational Problems in Children

Chapter **17**

The best indication that a psychologist, teacher or parent has about a child's learning ability or emotional well-being is in that child's performance. The difficulty that a child may have performing in an intelligent and well-organized manner in the classroom is rarely specific to that situation. Basically, classroom behavior can be seen as involving five categories of complex and integrative behaviors. A performance or educational problem can manifest itself in any or all of the five. In the classroom:

1. A child must be able to perceive the stimuli presented, be able to determine "what's demanded," and then have the ability to concentrate its attention on a specific problem or stimulus.
2. It must be able to organize incoming information in relation to past knowledge and then code it for future retrieval (memory).
3. A child must have some ability to communicate with others (language, verbal and written).
4. It must be motivated to perform (without performance there can be no indication that learning has taken place).
5. A child must display conduct appropriate to the situation. That is, he or she must "behave properly" as regards teacher and classmates.

None of these behaviors are restricted to the classroom. They are all demanded in the course of a child's everyday life. However, as the child must share the classroom with many children (and they are all there to experience a specific process, namely education) certain standards of behavior are defined. Behavior often ignored or tolerated at home may be more apparent and disruptive in school.

There is little data available for comparison, but experienced teachers have noted disturbed behavior is more common in the classroom today than it was twenty years ago. Several years ago, I participated in a classroom observational study at the University of Maryland. With two other observers, I sat at the back of a primary school classroom for one day, recording the quality of the teacher's response patterns. We rated each response the teacher made to a specific child (not to the class as a whole) as to whether it was instructive or disciplinary. On that day, we noted that *over 80 percent* of the teacher's interactions with individual children were of a disciplinary nature.

There are many factors accounting for the increase in educational problems today. The list includes: more comprehensive screening techniques, social permissiveness, changing values, dissolution of the family, urban stress, drugs and, of course, diet.*

Most people can understand that an extreme, unnatural diet can nurture emotional and disciplinary problems. We are less inclined to think that a child's diet can affect its learning ability. The sophistication with which learning disorders are now tested and treated is not matched by an awareness of what the child with a learning disorder is eating, and how that may affect his or her problem. For example, a child may be tested, diagnosed and classified as "dyslexic" (having a reading disorder). This is then seen as the problem and remedial reading is prescribed as the solution.

One expert on children with learning and emotional problems has written:

> When children who exhibit learning and/or behavioral disorders are examined by a number of specialists, the diagnosis is more closely related to the orientation of the specialist than it is to the essential problems of the child.
>
> A child may be ill because of a defect in his psychosocial environment or because of the biosocial environment or both may be in error.
>
> My experience leads me to conclude that in the vast majority of cases the error resides in the physical environment and usually in the nutrition and chemical airborne environment.[1]

---

*Food is often ignored as a basic factor in determining behavior. When an article in a leading weekly periodical begins, "Eleven-year-old Christopher Hansen swirled his grape lollipop in a glass of Pepsi..." and goes on to discuss discipline problems and unstable family relations without even considering the relationship of food and behavior...the perspective is limited. (*Newsweek,* May 15, 1978)

Of course, remedial reading and speech therapy can be helpful, but what of the child's diet? Often (not always) a child continues on a diet of chocolate, candy, soft drinks, chips, hot dogs, milk-shakes and processed, or "junk," foods.*

There is now evidence that the overall performance of high-school students' American college entrance examinations has been decreasing for the past fourteen years. Of course there are many factors to account for this decline including social factors, TV, curriculum changes and different student populations. One change that is usually ignored in discussing this problem is the unnatural, junk-food diet of today's young people. The habitual eating of junk foods and candy can lead to a condition where eating any sweets, even fruits and natural sweeteners, will be upsetting and reduce performance.

I have observed with some children that just eating a few candies, a piece of chocolate, some honey or a banana is sufficient to markedly decrease their reading ability.† After eating these foods, the children make more errors, their reading speed slows and their comprehension decreases.

There is now a growing recognition that the hyperactive child, the child with a learning disability, the "problem child," and even the child next door may be suffering from a serious bio-chemical disorder. Yet despite the extreme, unnatural eating habits of the children today, most experts advise a treatment for hyperactivity based on chemotherapy (usually *stimulants,* such as ritalin and dexadrine are prescribed) without any change in diet. Others recommend the elimination of a few specific foods such as sugar, foods with coloring and flavoring agents. I would suggest a marked reduction of all extreme and unnatural foods.

The same features of disintegration, alienation, insensitivity and extreme behavior that are a part of all contemporary problems can be found in the classroom. They can be reduced by living

---

*Junk foods are those that appeal to the taste, the eye, or the mind, but are not wholesome or nutritious.

†Bananas and dates are sweet palm fruits which can have an unbalancing effect on behavior, especially if people have a blood-sugar problem.

sensibly and eating well. In some cases, remedial instruction may be appropriate, and in most cases a child's internal state directly affects its behavior.

Children express a wide range of activity levels. I have lived and worked with some very active children whose behavior I considered healthy and normal. They may well have been "hyperactive" had not considerable attention been paid to ensure them a centered, natural diet.

In British Columbia, I was invited to address a group of teachers working with autistic and severely retarded children. After observing the children for several minutes, it was clear that each child was unique. Each had its own behavior pattern and many of the children were eating lots of refined carbohydrates and dairy food. There is no "magic diet" that can eliminate brain damage and severe retardation. Dietary change can, however, increase performance and help these children be more socialized. One could begin by eliminating all refined carbohydrates and chemical additives and decreasing dairy foods. Indeed, I have found that for almost all kinds of behavioral and emotional disturbances in children (and adults), a first step to establishing order and sanity is a change in diet.

THE FORMATIVE YEARS

Early life experiences, including early eating experiences, have a profound effect on all living beings. In fact, the closer one gets to conception, the greater is the significance of each and every stimulus in our development. It is well known that if a mother has an illness such as German measles during her early pregnancy, the child's development may be irreversibly affected. A similar effect may be the result of drugs (e.g., thalidomide) taken during pregnancy. In contrast, the same disease or drug will have a much less profound effect on a child or an adult. So it is with food.

The evolutionary time period required for a single-celled organism to evolve into a complex human being is said to be approximately three billion years. Yet, this process occurs within a female during the nine months of pregnancy. Accordingly, each day of pregnancy represents approximately ten million years of development. Hence a few days of a mother's chaotic eating, drinking and drug-taking can alter her internal environment and profoundly affect the fetus. It may even alter subsequent adult development and behavior.

Studies with animals and humans have shown that the quality of food in the earliest years has a greater impact than the same food eaten for an equal period later in life. It has been noted that if malnutrition extends through the most formative years of a child's mental development (from conception to age five), then retardation may be permanent. Severely malnourished children may experience an increase in I.Q. if their diets are enriched during this period.[2]

BRAIN FOOD

Brain damage and minimal brain dysfunction have become common problems of this age. Estimates are as high as one American child in 18 being affected by the latter. The causes are many and varied. Most fundamental is the biochemical environment of the fetus and child. Nothing is more basic to that milieu, and more controllable, than diet, especially the mother's diet during pregnancy and when nursing, and the child's diet after weaning.

Psychologists have noted the significance of early emotional experience on the development of the adult personality. The dispositions and attitudes of social behavior acquired in our first few years are those we'll most likely express throughout our lives. Similarly, the food a child eats in its formative years profoundly affects its later development and behavior. Of course, the idea that diet has its greatest impact in these early years does not mean its effect in later years is unimportant and can be ignored. The same principles of a centered, natural diet apply to young and old alike.

Perhaps the most dramatic example of how food can affect behavior occurs in the case of food-induced emotional reactions, or cerebral food allergies.

The food we eat is a basic factor determining our perceptions, attitudes and style of behaving. Its effects on us, though profound, are subtle, gradual and continuous. In most cases, it is the food eaten over a period of weeks, months, and years—even generations —that shapes our personalities. Some foods, however, cause an extreme, immediate and uncontrollable emotional reaction in *some* individuals. These reactions are the focus of this chapter.

Doctors and scientists have observed that some "normal" people react with uncontrollable anger, rage, crying and depression

Food-Induced Emotional Reactions

Chapter **18**

whenever they eat certain specific foods. When they avoid these foods they feel fine. Some experts consider these reactions to be "food allergies;" others—like myself—prefer to consider them food-induced emotional reactions (F.I.E.R.).

An account related to me by an elderly Montreal physician illustrates the profound consequences of F.I.E.R. and the relative misunderstanding of this phenomenon.

Some years before major tranquilizers were available, the doctor was a medical consultant to a large Montreal mental hospital. One day he was presented with the case of a patient who had a severe skin rash. The patient had been hospitalized for *over twenty years* for bizarre and disorderly behavior. To treat the rash, the physician prescribed some changes in the man's diet.

On returning to the hospital the following week, the doctor was enthusiastically received by the medical staff. They were anxious to know just what he had given the patient. Nothing at all, except for a change in diet, the doctor assured them. Then he asked about the rash, wanting to know if it had gotten worse. Quite the contrary, he was told—not only had the rash cleared up, but this man who had been severely disturbed for twenty years had suddenly become calm, communicative, rational and interested in his personal appearance. (Similar dramatic food-related behavior changes have been reported.)[1] The doctor went on to say, however, that for a few years he used diet a great deal in treatment of mental disorders; but then tranquilizers arrived on the scene and diet was once again ignored.

Clinics are now being established in America and Europe to determine which of those people suffering from inexplicable symptoms of emotional upset are food reactive and to what foods. Prior to testing, a suspected reactor is usually placed on a complete fast or a restricted diet for a few days. Then, the subject is exposed systematically to small quantities of a variety of food substances. The testing may be sublingual, placing a drop of the test food (in solution) under the tongue, or the food may be given to the subject in the normal manner. In both cases, the subject's reaction is observed and recorded. If an emotional reaction occurs, or there is a marked change in autonomic response (involuntary response patterns such as pulse, blood pressure, pupil dilatation), then a food-induced emotional reaction is suspected. Repeated testing is used to confirm the F.I.E.R. The reactive person is most frequently advised to avoid the reactive food. In other instances, he may be placed on a broad-spectrum restrictive diet.

The testing for F.I.E.R. has reduced the symptoms and suffering of many people and has helped to demonstrate a clear link between food and behavior. There are some limitations, however, to the approach as it is currently conceived. One is that the term food allergy (or cerebral food allergy) used by many of the experts suggests an abnormal and inappropriate sensitivity—a *disease process.* To the contrary, *many* of the foods commonly reported to lead to marked "allergic" reactions are sweets, sugar, chocolate, cow's milk and processed cheese, coffee, white bread and foods with chemical additives (especially artificial colors, flavors and preservatives). These are all foods which have previously been discussed as either extreme, disintegrating, alienating or unnatural. As such, they are often inappropriate and unnecessary. People reacting to these foods need not be considered "allergic," for that implies a maladaptive reaction to a wholesome food. Rather, they may be seen as hypersensitive to foods that have usually been chemically treated, refined and most often over-indulged in the past. The labeling of such sensitivity as a "food allergy" in many cases obscures the true nature of the disorder. Mothers worry about what to prepare and children—probably the most food-reactive group—worry about what to eat. Feeding the reactive individual natural whole foods would gradually eliminate many of their problems.

The whole problem of food-induced emotional reactions would be quite simple if it just involved a reaction to the inappropriate foods described. However, there are also a number of people who are reactive to *natural* foods such as cereal grains (especially wheat and corn), nuts and seeds. Some leading allergists have even suggested that a sensitivity to cereal grains is suspect in the majority of cases of mental illness.

The question most in need of being answered is: What is the most effective way(s) of treating food-induced emotional reactions?

WHAT TO DO ABOUT FOOD-INDUCED EMOTIONAL REACTIONS

At present, there are three basic approaches to treating food-induced emotional reactions:

- the restrictive diet approach
- the desensitization approach
- The metabolic approach

They reflect the different ways that experts see the problem and the most practical ways of dealing with it.

The Restrictive Diet Approach. Restricting the diet is probably the most common approach. Some people simply avoid the food they are sensitive to. Others are advised and follow a broad spectrum restrictive diet. The restrictive diets usually prescribed are high protein and low carbohydrate, but unlike the reducing diets mentioned earlier, they often advise the avoidance of chemically processed foods and food additives. This approach rarely makes a distinction between natural whole grains and chemically processed carbohydrates such as sugar, cake and commercial bread (you'll recall the latter may contain up to 40 chemical additives). People thought to be sensitive to white rice, cornmeal or wheat flour are often completely taken off all cereal grains.

One expert recommends what he calls a "stone-age diet." It consists of meat, fish, fresh fruit and vegetables. While this diet does eliminate processed foods and chemical additives, it is uncentering for it unnecessarily deprives many of all of the whole grains. This expert has said, "Our modern-day carbohydrate-based diet of *highly refined and processed foods contaminated by hundreds of newly invented synthetic chemicals* is such a recent innovation that there has not yet been time for extensive study of its effects on man. Most of the evidence beginning to come in, however, suggests the effects may be harmful."[2] While I agree that chemically treated, processed and highly refined carbohydrates (and other foods) may be a factor contributing to many behavior disorders, it does not follow to advise a diet eliminating all natural whole-cereal grains. Grain (chemically untreated and unrefined) has been the principal food for most of our species as we progressed from a stone-age mentality. As we continue to evolve, it seems inappropriate for man to revert to stone-age eating habits.

Some experts advise a restrictive diet (with or without additional treatment) as a temporary process to be followed until the sensitivity diminishes. Others, especially those who see the problem as a disease or "allergy," suggest a continuing restrictive diet as a way of life.

The Desensitization Approach. Desensitization is the second approach to treating F.I.E.R. Allergists in America and Europe make use of several different drugs (cortico-steroids, peptide blocking agents) and vaccines to accomplish this feat.

One London allergist has developed a vaccine to desensitize people to their allergies, including F.I.E.Rs.[3] During a day I spent with him in his clinic, I observed that many of his patients ate extreme diets with large quantities of refined carbohydrates, including sugar, dairy food and many chemically treated and processed foods. I suggested to him that these clients were intensifying their symptoms by eating these foods and thus increasing their reliance on pharmacology and repeated vaccination. He acknowledged this possibility and pointed out that many of these people would not be prepared to make basic changes in their diet and would experience social upset and considerable inconvenience because of their food reactivity. For many, therefore, desensitization provides a *convenient* and practical treatment approach although it may be one that nurtures and reinforces maladaptive and unde-sirable eating habits. It should be underlined that drugs like corti-sone and its derivatives used to reduce some allergic reactions, if taken habitually, have serious side effects, including irreversible metabolic changes, dependency, neurological changes and reduced carbohydrate tolerance.

The Metabolic Approach. The third approach to treating F.I.E.R. and the least symptomatic looks at these reactions as an expression of a more basic metabolic disorder.

To understand this approach, it is necessary to think a bit about metabolism and hypoglycemia. A healthy person is one who can digest and make use of what is eaten. If, for some reason, metabolism is upset and food can't be properly assimilated, behavior may become disordered. This is particularly true regarding the carbohydrates and hypoglycemia.

Hypoglycemia is a condition that has been associated with a whole range of serious behavior disorders. Recently, hypoglycemia has also been linked to "food allergies."[4] Experiments with animals demonstrate that all allergic reactions are worsened by low blood-sugar level and that some lethal ones will not occur at all if blood-sugar levels are normal. The same phenomenon has been reported in humans. Allergic individuals will no longer react to certain foods if their metabolism is reordered. This implies that many allergic and food-induced emotional reactions are reflections of a more basic metabolic disorder brought on by eating inappropriately.

I have observed in a number of cases that individuals who are sensitive or "allergic" to a certain food find their sensitivity to that food diminishes after a period of eating a centered, balanced, natural diet with *no overeating*.

In my own case, this approach has led to two beneficial results. First, it has made me less reactive to healthful, but previously "sensitizing" foods (such as wheat and corn) which I now enjoy. Second, it has enabled me to become more aware of those foods that reliably affect *my* mood and performance unfavorably (foods such as sugar, sweets, peanut butter, and foods with MSG*). I now avoid these foods.

Food testing is one effective way of discriminating which foods can elicit a F.I.E.R. But remember, your reactivity to these foods (like your performance) is not always constant. By changing your diet—eliminating many extreme, refined, and unnatural foods—and not overeating, you can become less reactive to previously upsetting healthful foods, and more aware of those foods you had really best avoid.

A note on eating grain: A number of people have remarked that cereal grains "don't agree with them." They report that grains cause acidity, heaviness, indigestion and mucous. No doubt *some* people are reactive or sensitive to whole grains. However, I have found that the three *primary* causes of indigestion associated with eating cereal grains are (1) eating too much grain (or anything else); (2) not chewing grains thoroughly; and (3) the common practice of eating foods with grains that do not combine well with them. This is especially true of mixing grains with sweets, fruits and fats. Such old-time favorites as the peanut butter and jelly sandwich, bagels and cream cheese, combination pizzas and chocolate brownies are all poor combinations. Cereal grains should be eaten in sensible proportions, chewed well and combined wisely with all foods.

One food expert suggested a two-sided explanation of why F.I.E.R.s are triggered by both refined carbohydrates (sugar, candy, soda pop, cookies, white bread, etc.) and natural whole carbohydrates (like whole wheat, corn, brown rice, etc.).[6] He saw the reaction to the refined, chemically processed carbohydrates as a hypersensitivity or intolerance to what was inappropriate and had been overindulged in the past. In contrast, the reaction to whole, untreated carbohydrates was an expression of a disordered

---

*MSG, monosodium glutamate, is a taste enhancer which is used in many foods (soups, desserts, Chinese food). MSG has been associated with a wide range of physical and behavioral symptoms. It specifically affects the hypothalamus (an area responsible for controlling appetite). Children are especially sensitive to its effects.[5]

metabolism that resulted from eating too many of the first kind of foods and which inhibited normal food processing.

He suggested that both could be dealt with in the same manner —by avoiding *all refined* carbohydrates, sweets and chemically processed foods and by adopting a centered diet of natural whole foods. When I asked him what happens if an individual reacts to whole grains, he suggested that they should be *gradually* reintroduced into the diet along with plenty of vegetables (especially greens) and that the person chew very well and avoid overeating.

This advice is consistent with some recent findings that natural whole-grain diets (centered) are an effective way of treating hypoglycemia.*[7] Previously, it has been thought that high-protein/low-carbohydrate diets were most effective. The apparent contradiction exists because advocates of the low-carbohydrate diet didn't distinguish between whole natural carbohydrates and refined processed carbohydrates. It's the latter that are disordering.

To summarize, there are three techniques for dealing with food-induced emotional reactions. The restrictive diet approach generally assumes the person is allergic and should avoid the reactive food. The desensitization approach focuses on removing the symptom (with medication) and not changing the diet. Lastly, the metabolic approach attempts to reduce sensitivity by improving metabolic function. It stresses the importance of eating properly. Some, like myself, generally advise a centered whole grain-based diet; others advise a low carbohydrate or extreme diet. In all cases, motivation is similar—to eliminate F.I.E.R. and restore normal behavior.

An elderly gentleman I worked with in Greece was well into his eighties, yet he displayed the energy and vitality of a much

---

*I generally advise hypoglycemics to eat whole grains and vegetables (specifically greens and sweet vegetables, like carrots, and squash) as part of a centered, natural diet (no sugar, low fat). I also recommend they avoid overeating, and exercise a good deal regularly. It is sometimes appropriate to eat a little more high-protein foods in the initial stages of this diet.

younger man. I mentioned my interest in food and behavior and then inquired about his dietary habits. He told me that he ate everything, albeit in small quantities. When I asked him what advice he might pass on he smiled and replied, "None." Then, after a moment's silence he added, "There is one thing. If I eat something and it makes me sick, I don't usually eat it again."

An ideal of eating well is being (or becoming) sufficiently sensitive and self-aware that you can appreciate which foods contribute to your well-being and which affect you adversely. The latter should be avoided.

FOOD PREPARATION AND ATTITUDES

Section **V**

Cooking is a contractive process. When you apply energy in the form of heat to your food, it contracts. Vegetables, meat, fish and fruit all shrink in size when cooked. Cooking also has a contractive effect on behavior.

Most people eat both raw and cooked food. A few, however, eat cooked or raw foods exclusively. I have lived with and counseled both of these extreme groups and have observed a basic difference in their behavior. Basically, raw eaters are expansive. They are more spontaneous, talkative and emotional (they tend to laugh and cry more easily). They also enjoy movement and move about more than their cooked-eating counterparts. Sometimes, though, they lack direction and self-control.

The behavior of cooked-food eaters is more contractive. They tend to be more controlled, less emotional and less permissive.

Raw or Cooked?

Chapter **19**

Cooked-food eaters also tend to be somewhat more conceptual, traditional and time conscious than raw eaters. Differential effects of raw versus cooked foods are shown in the following table. These differences cannot be attributed solely to the way these groups prepare their food. Cooked eaters also tend to eat a diet of foods that is somewhat more contractive than what most raw eaters eat.

RAW FOODS	COOKED FOODS
More expansive	More contractive
Alkalizing, cleansing	Generally more acid-forming
Particularly effective after extreme diet (meat-sweet) and extreme life-style; *reduces acidosis*	Cooking makes high-fiber foods such as grains and root vegetables more easily digested
Behaviorally, nurtures more spontaneous, talkative, emotional and physical activity	Nurtures more intellectual, conceptual thinking, and less of a physical mentality; develops inhibition*
Primary foods are fruits, salads, vegetables, sprouts; some dairy possible	Generally a more contractive diet; grains, beans, salt; some animal products possible

*Inhibition is an active neurological and psychological process that enables an organism to have greater response selectivity and control.

These two patterns—cooking everything or eating everything raw—represent the extremes. Most of us eat somewhere in-between. You can best determine how much cooking to do by appreciating your needs and circumstances. Raw food is most appropriate in tropical regions and warm seasons where the sun is hot and where more expansive behavior is required. A greater proportion of foods need to be cooked in colder, more contractive regions and seasons (winter) when contractive behavior is most appropriate.

The correct cooking formula is something you have to decide for yourself. In general, it appears when practical circumstances (region, season, vocation and constitution) demand contraction, then food is prepared by increasing the variables of heat, pressure and time and decreasing the amount of fluid. When circumstances demand expansion, preparation consists of reducing the heat, pressure and time and using more fluid. In mid-winter in Great Britain or New England, it follows that raw eating would be limited whereas in southern California or Mexico, less cooking is required, especially in summer.

My own diet consists of about 35 to 50 percent whole grain, most of which is cooked. While living in the tropics, in the desert and during summer, I cook less and eat more raw food (e.g., salads and fruits) than when I'm living in colder times and places.

THEORIES ABOUT COOKING

Cooking is a form of food processing, one that can increase or reduce the food energy available to us. Some raw-food advocates suggest that we should eat just raw food. They maintain that cooking destroys the life energy in food and that the introduction of fire into food preparation signalled the beginning of the deterioration of man's health.

In contrast, there are those who advocate that cooking was one of the prime factors that enabled mankind to transcend our animal nature.

There is no clear record of humans before they knew the use of fire... [just] as the habit of erect posture and walking on two legs alone freed the hands for delicate skills, so the use of fire for cooking...freed the face for its intricate task of communication (by reduction of chewing structures, changes in the brain case gave the brain room for growth). [1]

Cooked-food eaters counter arguments that cooking destroys life energy with the suggestion that in cooking, energy is put into food in the form of fire and pressure and thus the energy of the food is increased.

Swiss and Danish philosophers have expressed the view that cooking can be used to liberate the life energy in food. Generally, the minimum of cooking is desired, but this varies with the part of the plant to be used.[2] As shown in the illustration below, the fruit and blossoms (1) directly exposed to the sun are most easily digestible and require no cooking. The stalk and leaves (2) are considerably less digestible than the fruits and blossoms and require some cooking, while those of the roots (3) and blossomless fruits (grains) require even more preparation.

Similarly, nutritionists have observed that cooking is far more destructive to the vitamin content (vitamins A and C) in fruit, for which it is unnecessary, than in grains, beans, and root vegetables.

An Indian yogi I visited put it another way.[3] He said that raw fruits were fine, but that root vegetables can be difficult to digest if uncooked.*

---

*The yogic diet considers several root vegetables (like onion and radish) "rajasic" or disturbing to the mind and inner peace.

DON'T OVERCOOK

Cooking has differential effects on food and behavior. Raw foods stimulate physical action and spontaneity. Cooked foods nurture conceptual thinking, the ability to organize. Cooking can be helpful and healthful, especially for those foods such as grains, beans and root vegetables which are difficult to digest when raw. However, *overcooking should be avoided.*

It is advised that only the minimal amount of energy necessary and the most subtle cooking medium be employed in the preparation of food.* Some recently popularized kitchen devices (e.g., microwave ovens and food processors) save time and effort, and brutalize and destroy the food. Excessive and insensitive food preparation decreases food energy and reduces vitality.

---

*Generally, the most desirable cooking utensils are those that are least reactive (do not chemically interact) with the food. Stainless steel, clay and glass cookware are fine. Enamel is also fine provided it is of good quality and the enamel does not flake off into the food. More reactive and less desirable is aluminum cookware, which may react visibly with very reactive foods (e.g., spinach, tomato, rhubarb), and some of the chemically-coated cooking utensils.

A woman cooking
stands unnoticed
stirring the elements
drawing power to transform.
Alchemy everyday
at each meal
an expectation
satisfying others
nurturing
creative instincts.

A woman cooking
(unnoticed)
the family center
in an apron
of beauty and power.

S.M.

Attitudes
When Cooking
and Eating

Chapter **20**

Cooking is alchemy in daily life. It is a transformation of energy that requires the ability to organize and manipulate the elements fire, water, air and earth. Cooking is the highest development of an art. It is an art that creates and sustains life as well as one that celebrates it as do painting, drama, literature, music and dance.

In some cultures, cooking was appreciated as an area of supreme creative expression that could profoundly affect the health and consciousness of the family or community. For example, in the Zen monasteries of Japan the responsibility of cooking was frequently given to one of the more respected or senior monks. *Syozin ryori,* which means cooking that develops higher judgement, was an ideal to be realized. Developing the art of cooking, like most skills, requires time, discipline, motivation and some social or cultural support.

In most countries, the mother does the cooking. This may correlate with the almost universal (transhistorical, transcultural) consideration of woman as "mother earth." Of course food can be prepared with sensitivity by both sexes. Indeed, most restaurant chefs are men. What is probably more important than *who* does the cooking is *how* the food is prepared.

THE COOK'S ATTITUDE

It is a widely held belief of peoples throughout the world that you can eat the food prepared by someone with a healthy, even disposition, but you should avoid the food of a sick, angry or frightened cook.

A friend who is a psychic researcher in England showed me a series of Kirlian photographs he had taken demonstrating the effect of different attitudes on food. When the food (in this case, cooked cauliflower) was touched by someone who was angry, the size and brightness of the photographed aura (an indication of the energy released) was considerably less than when it was touched "with love."[1] Though many people have demonstrated how the human aura varies with a change in emotion, I have *not* been able to replicate this effect when food was involved. I have, however, taken Kirlian photographs of several different breads which demonstrate that "home-baked" breads have more energy than the popular mass-produced commercial variety. Many believe, as I do, that there is a special ingredient in some homemade food which, though difficult to quantify, can affect behavior and overall well-being. It has been my experience that most restaurants, caterers and hostesses cook for taste and appearance rather than for health. (Good cooking takes everything into account.) Over the years, I have developed a decided preference for my wife's or my own natural homemade fare. I rarely "eat out." My researcher friend who dines in restaurants every day says that before eating he always takes the precaution of making a cross over his food "just to neutralize what went on in the kitchen."

The attitude that surrounds food may at times be as important as the actual substance of the food itself. There is a story of a Japanese philosopher and teacher with rather definite views on diet which included the idea that eating sugar leads to disorder and disease. He was visiting the home of some of his students, brothers who had impressed him as young men of fine character. He particularly wanted to meet their mother, for he felt that the mother of such fine sons must be a remarkable woman. One of the sons reminded his mother of the teacher's visit and suggested that it might be a good idea if she removed everything containing sugar from sight. Much to the later dismay of this student, his philosopher-teacher is said to have discovered in some kitchen corner a freshly baked batch of sugar cookies. The student tried to explain away the cookies, but his teacher would have none of it. "Nonsense," he exclaimed, "these cookies were made with love. I will eat them all."[2]

THE FAMILY THAT
EATS TOGETHER

Traditionally, members of a family ate the same food. The family blood, body chemistry and well-being were regulated by the cook (usually the mother), who provided one diet for all. Present-day families are disintegrating and experiencing serious communication problems between family members. Diet is a basic ingredient in this family stew.

Last year, I spent a few days visiting an internationally famous psychiatric clinic in the American Midwest. I was surprised to find that no one on staff specialized, researched or even seemed particularly interested in the relationship between food and mental health. Furthermore, there were soft-drink and candy machines scattered around for the use of patients and staff.

I requested, and was granted, interviews with three senior psychiatrists—gentlemen who had been around for enough time to have observed the changing pattern of diet in America. I asked them if they felt that modern-day eating habits contributed to mental illness and, if so, how? They all agreed that the way we eat can affect our behavior. Their focus, however, was directed more to the social aspects of eating than to what people actually ate. One psychiatrist remarked, "The family doesn't eat together anymore." The dinner table used to be a place around which a family gathered and were a family, but that's no longer the case.

Today it's routine for people to "grab a bite" of some mass-produced, instant food whenever and wherever it's convenient. The National Restaurant Association estimates that one out of every three meals in the U.S. is now eaten away from home and, by 1980, it will rise to one out of every two.[3] Moreover, the meals eaten at home are increasingly of the fast, frozen and pre-prepared variety. These trends are being reflected in family relations.

One writer described the fragmentation of the American family and its dietary habits as follows:

*In the twentieth century, family could be characterized as a group having the
same address and telephone number. During the first days of life, the infant
feeds via a hospital assembly line. Then sugared meals come out of
supermarket jars. Before children have developed judgment other than at the
tip of their tongues, brother and sister feed themselves with toasted waffles
out of a box, pancakes out of a jug. The words treat and snack are drained
of meaning; the children treat themselves when the impulse moves them:*
At the refrigerator, the freezer, the candy store,
the school cafeteria, the vending machine.

*Mother takes her weight watcher's concoctions out of a box; downtown,
Daddy has a two-martini, credit-card lunch. Kids spoil their suppers with
supermarket snacks and sugared drinks. If frozen TV dinners on individual
trays are too much for mother, if she deserves a break today, the family
rattles off to the nearest drive-in, where it's each his own.* [4]

WILLIAM DUFTY, *SUGAR BLUES*

Like the family, religious groups and communities have,
throughout the ages, maintained their cohesiveness through their
dietary habits. Still today, many Jews, Mormons, Moslems, Bud-
dhists, Hindus and Sikhs follow a strict dietary code.

There is now some scientific evidence that community and
presumably family cohesiveness is influenced by diet. Several
years ago, I participated in a physiological investigation of 210
members of the Boston "macrobiotic" community.* The study
revealed that community members had blood pressure significantly
lower than the general public (a reliable finding amongst vegetarians). What was as interesting, however, was the finding that
community members, including those living in separate houses,
all had *aggregated* blood pressure. That is to say, there was a significant clustering of blood pressure amongst all of the unrelated
members of the community tested. [5] Since members of the community represented different ages, sexes, races, religions and

---

*Macrobiotics eat a centered, grain-based diet.

educational backgrounds, one of the only factors common to all was the centered diet of the community.

The phenomenon of aggregated blood pressure noted in this study had only been observed previously in families in relation to first-degree relatives, spouses and often amongst "less civilized" peoples eating a more simple (centered, natural whole-food) diet. It seems that the family that eats together, and eats simply, is in harmony with each other.

A NOTE ON POLITICS AND FOOD

Just as diet influences family and community feelings, it affects the thinking and action of the masses. Indeed, it has been said that the fate of nations depends on the way they eat.

I was once asked by a reporter, "If politicians ate differently, would their politics change?" I replied that a change in diet can influence anyone's chemistry and that one's chemistry can shape and influence behavior. I also explained to him that he could be trained to look or listen to a political figure, or anyone for that matter, and determine what that person has been eating or eating too much of.

An awareness of the significance of a healthy diet for political well-being goes way back. Almost a thousand years ago it was written, "A king that cannot rule him[self] in his diet will hardly rule his realm in peace and quiet."[6]

On a broader scale, the rise and fall of nations and waves of political influence have been directly related to food. One expert wrote:

> *Anthropologists everywhere ask why the centers of achievement and power pass from people to people although the racial stock and geography remain relatively constant. Nutrition might furnish the answer.*[7]

Waves of political influence can be seen simply as waves of expansion and contraction, and these movements can be related to a few basic factors, including diet.

RECOMMENDATIONS

Section **VI**

An aspiring and health-conscious young man sought the counsel of a visiting sage, who he heard, had a special diet for health and longevity. He waited for hours to see the old wise man and learn his secret. Finally his turn came. Rather earnestly, he asked the sage, "What is the magic diet?" The old man looked at him for a minute and said patiently, "What you eat depends on knowing who you are and what you may want from life."

I rarely prescribe a fixed diet—especially impersonally. Everyone is unique and everything is changing. Yet, "a diet" is static and as such it can be unbalancing and restrictive. Indeed, most diets designed to re-establish order are restrictive and many are neither centered nor balanced. Frequently they advise one class of foods (e.g., protein) and exclude another (e.g., carbohydrates) without any appreciation or explanation of balance (expansion-contraction). The result is still more disorder. People report cravings, hunger, bingeing and preoccupation with food as well as irritability, anger and emotional upset.

Recommendations

Chapter **21**

If you are eating in a balanced way and your diet is appropriate, you will feel well and enjoy your food. Even young children will regulate themselves and their diets, especially if they can be made to appreciate through *their own experience* that eating certain foods leads to their feeling well while eating other foods leads to feeling upset.[1] A person who enjoys his or her food *and its effects* will not be a "diet cheater." The craving to be eating something else is often a sign of imbalance. It may sometimes accompany the initial stages of a healthy readjustment (change, even healthy change, can sometimes feel uncomfortable and strange), but if it persists, something is missing or "not right."

Some people coming for counseling are not really interested in becoming more centered and self-regulating. Rather, they want a pill, a magic formula or a special food that would allow them to carry on pretty much as they were before. On the other hand, many people are motivated to change their lifestyle and dietary habits, but don't know where to begin.

Social psychologists have observed that people learn most effectively by first observing a model in a situation and then experiencing that situation for themselves. Unfortunately, available models, such as parents and television commercials, often do not provide appropriate stimuli or direction. In the 10,000 food-related television commercials that American children watch each year, they observe spacemen, sportsmen, entertainers, father figures, mother figures, beauties, cartoon characters, he-men, the kid next door and anyone else with whom one can identify giving incorrect information about food.[2] For example, they say that chemical breakfast drinks and sugary refined cereals are healthful, and the best thing for a child beginning his day...or, that artificial taste powders bring out the real taste qualities in the food. Others lure people into eating uncentered and unnatural foods by promising greater health, attractiveness and pleasure.

Over $1,150,000,000 is spent annually in the United States on the television advertising of food and it has been estimated that about 80 percent of that food is *un*healthy.[3] With six of the ten leading causes of *death* in the United States being linked directly to food, there's need for a new and sane approach to diet.[4]

WHAT TO EAT

What follows are five recommendations on what to eat. They are based on the inter-relation of food and behavior that has been described in this book and are consistent with the latest findings and dietary policies.[5]

Basically, I advise eating a centered, natural diet and avoiding extreme, disintegrating and alienating foods. The *five recommendations* for a sane and satisfying diet are:

1. Eat centered foods.
2. Avoid the extremes—that means low meat, low sweet and low fat.
3. Remember the law of opposites.
4. Eat naturally.
5. Avoid overeating.

Let me elaborate briefly on these recommendations:

Eat Centered Foods. By centered foods I mean cereal grains, vegetables, fruits, nuts and beans (all the seed plants).
  Cereal Grains: The cereal grains are:

- *Rice*—that's natural brown rice, not polished, instant or white rice.
- *Whole Wheat*—most frequently eaten as bread and pasta, though it is also eaten as cracked wheat, farina and bulghur. It should always be 100 percent whole and free from additives, preservatives and sweeteners. Bread is *not* the best way to eat grain, especially for people with intestinal problems. The yeastiness of bread (even whole wheat bread) is more difficult for the intestines to process than grain in other forms.

Substituting or adding *rye* to bread may be a good idea, especially if you have a weight problem.

Wheat-sensitive individuals can substitute millet, rice or buckwheat (the latter is not related to wheat) in place of wheat.

- *Millet*—a fine yellow grain that's said to be especially good for people with blood-sugar problems.
- *Buckwheat*—usually eaten as kasha (groats), buckwheat flour in pancakes and crepes or as noodles (soba). It's a good cold-weather grain.
- *Oats*—usually ground into meal or rolled into flakes for oat-meal and porridge; avoid instant oats.
- *Barley*—another grain that can be used in baking, in soups (a personal favorite) or on its own.
- *Corn* (maize)—eaten as cornmeal, cornbread and tortilla.

Generally, I recommend that about a third of one's diet consist of *whole* cereal grains. As you can see, these grains can be eaten in many forms and at any "meal." Grains are the staff of life. Don't confuse the cereal grains with the breakfast "cereals" most of which are loaded with sugar, preservatives and chemical additives and are best avoided.

Vegetables: Eat a variety of fresh vegetables. Most vegetables are fine, especially those in season. You can prepare them in a variety of ways: steamed, baked, sautéed or raw in salads. Remember, vegetables lose their vitality if overcooked...especially greens.

Fruits: Eat seasonal and regional fruits, but not in excess. Fresh fruit is fine; Candied fruit and sugar preserved fruit are not. Dried fruit is best in winter. Fruits are most suitable to warm weather; too much fruit in the winter is expansive and will make you more sensitive to the cold.

Nuts: Some nuts and beans are also part of a centered diet. Almonds, walnuts, hazelnuts and pecans are fine. Less preferable are brazils, cashews, pistachios and peanuts. Nuts should be eaten plain, and in moderation. Avoid nut butters and nuts prepared with salt and vegetable oils. Seeds, like nuts, are fine in moderation, especially sesame, sunflower, and pumpkin seeds.

Beans: Black, white, pink, red, yellow, striped, lentils and chickpeas (garbanzos) are all centered foods. Eat them if you enjoy them. However, beans should be well-prepared (it's advisable to presoak them and cook them at least one hour); otherwise, they can be difficult to digest. Tofu (soybean curd) can be used in place of dairy food in many dishes. Beans can also be sprouted providing a source of fresh food (especially in winter).

These centered foods should comprise *at least 85 percent* of your diet. Of course, eating a centered diet means eating *less extreme food*—less salt, meat, eggs, sugar, sweets, coffee, soda pop and alcohol.

Avoid the Extremes. *Eat a low-meat diet.* To be more specific, reduce the quantity of extreme contractive food that you eat. *Meat,* eggs and cheese are very contractive and concentrated foods. As such they can be unbalancing and desensitizing. When eaten, these foods should be fresh and preferably free from chemicals.

Salt should only be used sparingly. It is extremely contractive and should be avoided by small children, pregnant women, old folks and those with hypertension and high blood pressure. When salt is used, it should be sea salt (see page 56).

Eat a low sweet diet. Sugar and *sweets,* including candy, chocolate, cookies, cakes, molasses, honey and anything containing sugar (white or brown) are best avoided, especially by those with blood-sugar problems, heart disease and those prone to emotional instability, depression and hyperactivity. Soft drinks or soda pop should also be avoided. Either they're full of sugar or they're full of chemical sweeteners.

Coffee and alcohol are also extreme expansive foods with an extreme effect on the nervous system and behavior.

Eat a low fat diet. Whether it's animal or vegetable, saturated or unsaturated, all fatty food cuts down your circulation, reduces your sensitivity, increases your weight and generally contributes to your feeling less vital and less attractive. Eggs, cheese, butter, fatty meats, peanut butter, margarine and fried foods are best eaten only sparingly.

Remember the Law of Opposites. Expansion balances contraction. Meat leads to sweet (and alcohol). It's the dynamics of sane eating. Understanding this law gives you greater insight and control in balancing and centering your diet and your behavior.

Eat Naturally. Whenever possible eat fresh, whole food. That includes: whole grains, vegetables, fruits, nuts, beans and animal produce raised in a wholesome manner.

Eat fresh and homemade food rather than canned, instant or pre-prepared foods. About the only way to be sure of the ingredients and the quality of the food you eat is to prepare it at home *starting from the basics.* Make your own soups, bake your own bread and cookies, sprout your own sprouts.

Avoid unnatural (disintegrated, chemicalized) food. Whenever possible eat food that is grown *without chemical treatment* (pesticides, herbicides, soil fumigants are upsetting to us as well as the bugs). Similarly, whenever possible, eat food free of chemical additives (e.g., artificial colors, flavors and preservatives). There are 3,000 chemical additives in use today and many of them have been shown to cause disorders in laboratory animals and man. It's advisable to read labels carefully.

Avoid refined foods. Sugar and white flour are not part of a sane diet. Remember, sugar is hidden in most commercial foods. To reduce your craving for sweets, eat more fresh vegetables and fruits and salads, and less of those extreme contractive foods that will attract you to sweets.

Eat food you enjoy. However, try to develop your judgement by avoiding extreme, spicy and artificially flavored foods. They distort your senses and ultimately your judgement. Low-quality favorite tastes for such foods will disappear with a little discipline as you re-educate your sense of taste.

As this is a book about food, I have said little about the behavioral consequences of alcohol, tobacco, drugs, coffee and diet pills. Like sweets, they all unbalance and fatigue the nervous system and should be avoided.

Avoid Overeating. Quantity destroys quality. A major cause of disease is simply eating too much. Similarly, avoid eating too many foods at any one time. A balanced diet does not mean eating a little of everything at one meal. Eat simply.

To summarize, what's recommended, is a *centered, natural* diet.

Centered means:

- a low-meat, low-sweet, low-fat diet.
- a low-salt, sugar-free, caffeine-free diet.

Natural means:

- an unrefined, unadulterated, whole-food diet.
- a high-fiber diet.

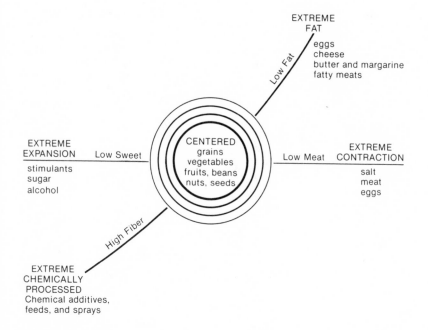

As for how to eat, see Chapter 15 (pages 127–132) and remember to take your time, eat slowly and chew your food well. Do not try to change yourself overnight, or in a week. You have a lifetime...begin today.

These general recommendations will provide a sound basis for your self-experimentation. They are designed to help you become more sane, satisfied and attractive.

As I've said throughout this book, food is just one factor that accounts for human variability and affects our mental and physical health. Along with eating a sane diet, it is important to be mentally and physically active, to relax effectively, to have a positive attitude or direction and to be able to enjoy and learn from life.

The saying, "Man does not live by bread alone" does not mean that food is unimportant. It is basic. A centered, natural diet is a beginning.

Chapter 1 Introduction

[1]From *Man, The Unknown* by Alexis Carrel, New York: Harper & Row, 1935, p. 87. Copyright 1935, 1939 by Harper & Row, Publishers, Inc.; renewed 1967 by Anne De La Motte Carrel. Reprinted by permission of Harper & Row, Publishers, Inc.

Chapter 2 Food: A Total View

[1]Protein: carbohydrate ratio can be calculated from data found in *Composition of Foods*, B.K. Watt & A.L. Merrill, U.S. Department of Agriculture Handbook, Number 8, U.S. Government Printing Office, Washington, D.C., 1975.

Chapter Notes

Chapter 4   Man's Principal Food

[1]Biblical references are taken from *The Holy Bible,* Authorized (King James) Version.

[2]From *The Scotsman's Food* by K.H. Kitchen and R. Passemore, Edinburg: E. & S. Livingston, 1947.

[3]Three books that provide interesting information and entertaining reading are: *The Foodbook* by James Trager, New York: Avon Books, 1972; *Food in History* by Reay Tannahill, London: Eyre Methuen, 1973; *The Oxford Book of Food Plants,* by S.G. Harrison et al., Oxford: Oxford University Press, 1969.

Chapter 6   Centering

[1]*Hara* by K.G. Von Durkheim, London: G. Allen & Unwin Ltd., 1962.

[2]*The Lonely Crowd* by D. Reisman, New Haven, Conn.: Yale University Press, 1961.

[3]*Dietary Goals for the United States,* Select Committee on Nutrition and Human Needs (U.S. Senate), U.S. Government Printing Office, Washington, D.C., 1977.

[4]Cognitive Effects of False Heart Rate Feedback by S. Valins, *Journal of Personality and Social Psychology, 4,* 1966, p. 468.

[5]A popular food combination reference is *Food Combination Made Easy* by H. Shelton, San Antonio, Texas: Shelton Press, 1951.

[6]The two accounts relating food to the sufi way of life are taken from the writings of Idres Shah: *Caravan of Dreams,* Baltimore, Md: Penguin Books, 1968; *The Way of the Sufi,* London, Jonathan Cape, 1964.

Chapter 7   Extremes

[1]*The Vegetable Passion* by J. Barkas, New York: Scribner, 1975.

[2]Based on statistics reported by the Los Angeles coroner in 1977.

[3]Japanese expressions used in *Food for Thought* have been corroborated by Michio Kushi and Yoshio Kawahara, Japanese friends and teachers.

[4]From *Food and Man* by M.E. Lowenberg et al., New York: John Wiley, 1968.

[5]*In the Shadow of Man* by Jane V.L. Goodall, Boston: Houghton Mifflin, 1971.

[6]The physiological effects of an extreme, high-meat diet can be found in diverse sources: Blood Pressure in Vegetarians by F. Sarks, B. Rosner & E. Kass, *Am. J. Epid., 100* (5), 1976, pp. 390–398; The Relation of Protein Foods to Hypertension, by A.N. Donaldson, *Calif. W. Med., 24,* 1926, pp. 328–330; Effect of Diet in Essential Hypertension by F. Hatch et al., *Am. J. Med, 17,* 1954, pp. 499–513; Diet and Blood Pressure by S. Jejda et al., *Lancet, 1,* 1967, p. 1103; Effects of the Rice Diet upon the Blood Pressure of Hypertensive Individuals by H.A. Schroeder et. al., *Ann. Inter. Med., 30,* 1949, pp. 712–732; *The Save Your Life Diet* by D. Reuben, New York: Random House, 1975; *Food Is Your Best Medicine* by H. Bieler, New York: Random House, 1966; Dr. Bieler is critical of the high-protein diet, especially its adverse effects on the kidneys and liver; *Live Longer Now* by J.N. Leonard, J.L. Hofer and N. Pritikin, New York: Grosset & Dunlap, 1971 (A centered diet low in extreme foods—salt, meat and sweets—is advised to eliminate and prevent a variety of degenerative diseases.); *The Word of Wisdom: A Modern Interpretation* by J. and L. Widstoe, Salt Lake City: Deseret, 1950 (The authors discuss Mormon dietary policy, which includes the idea of eating meat sparingly. They also cite Pavlov's research on liver bypasses in dogs, which reported that "bypassed" dogs fed vegetarian diets lived significantly longer than those fed carnivorous diets.); *World Keys to Health and Long Life* by Bernard Gensen, Escondido, Calif: Omni Publications, 1975 (Examines the diet of Longevity.); Arthritis and Diet by N. Pritikin, Santa Barbara, Calif.: August 1977.

[7]Miami Herald, June 29, 1976.

[8]The influence of nutrients on the intake of alcohol by U.D. Registrar, *J. American Dietetic Assoc., 61,* 1972, p. 159; *Nutrition Against Disease* by R.J. Williams, New York: Pitman, 1971; High carbohydrate diet affects rats' alcohol intake, *J. American Medical Assoc., 212,* 1970, p. 976.

Chapter 8   Overexpansion, Overcontraction

[1] *The Complete Illustrated Book of Yoga* by Swami Vishnudevananda, New York: Julian Press, 1960.

Chapter 9   Balancing Perspectives

[1] A considerable amount has been written about fasting: *Fasting, the Ultimate Diet* by Allen Cott, New York: Bantam Books, 1975; *Fasting for Renewal of Life* by H. Shelton, Chicago: Natural Hygiene Press, 1974; *Rational Fasting* by Arnold Ehret, Lust Publications, 1971; *Journal of a Fast* by Frederick Smith, New York: Schocken Books, 1976.

[2] From *The Gospel of Peace of Jesus Christ* translated and edited by Edmond Szekely, London: C.W. Daniel, 1973, p. 43.

[3] From *Porphyry on Abstinence from Animal Food* translated by T. Taylor, edited by W. Taylor. London: Barnes & Noble Books, 1965 (An interesting book taken from the 3rd century writings of the great scholar.).

[4] *Bliss Devine* by Swami Sivananda (M.D.), India: Divine Life Society, 1974.

[5] Betty Shepherd, London, 1975.

[6] *Human Nutrition* by J. Meyer, Springfield, Ill.: Thomas, 1962.

[7] Nutrition and heart disease, a preventative programme by T. Murray, *J. Canadian Dietetic Assoc., 39,* 1978, pp. 6–10.

Chapter 10   Dis-Integration

[1] Two books I'd recommend are: *The Saccharine Disease* by T.L. Cleve, Bristol: John Wright and Sons Ltd., 1974; *The Save Your Life Diet* by D. Reuben, New York: Random House, 1975.

[2] See, Wartime changes in admission for Schizophrenia by F.C. Dohan, *Acta Psychiatria Scandinavia, 42,* 1966, p. 125.

[3]Study carried out by Sir Robert McCarrison. See *Nutrition and Health* by R. McCarrison and H.M. Sinclair, London: Faber, 1964.

[4]There have been several books written on the adverse physical effects of eating low-fiber, refined foods. The list includes: *Refined Carbohydrate Foods and Disease* by D.P. Burkitt and H.C. Trowell, London: Academic Press, 1975; *Nutrition Against Disease* by R.J. Williams, New York: Pitman, 1971; *The Saccharine Disease* and *The Save Your Life Diet* referred to in the first note.

[5]Graph taken from Dietary Goals for the United States, U.S. Government Printing Office, Washington, D.C.: 1977, p. 26.

[6]*Psychodietetics* by E. Cheraskin and W.M. Ringsdorf, New York: Stein & Day, 1974.

[7]See *Nutrition Against Disease* by R.J. Williams, New York: Pitman, 1971; *Mental and Elemental Nutrients* by C. Pfeiffer, New Canaan, Conn.: Keats, 1975; *Psycho-nutrition* by C. Fredricks, New York: Grosset & Dunlap, 1976.

[8]Orthomolecular psychiatry by L. Pauling, *Science,* 19, April 19, 1968, pp. 263–271.

[9]From *Remember to Remember* by Henry Miller, New York: New Directions, 1961.

[10]Conducted at Schiller College, London, England, November 1975.

[11]*Ego, Hunger and Aggression* by F. Perls, New York: Vintage Books, 1969.

[12]Ibid. p. 116.

Chapter 11   Sugar

[1]Several of the interesting books written about sugar and its destructive properties include: *Sugar Blues* by William Dufty, Radnor, Pa.: Chilton Books, 1975; *Pure White and Deadly* by J. Yudkin, London: Davis Paynter Ltd., 1972 (published in the United States as *Sweet and Dangerous,* New York: Bantam Books, 1972); *Body, Mind and Sugar* by E. Abrahamson and A.W. Pezet, New York: Pyramid Books, 1971.

[2]*Natural Health, Sugar and the Criminal Mind* by J.I. Rodale, New York: Pyramid Books, 1968; *Hypoglycemia, Low Blood Sugar and You* by C. Fredericks and H. Goodman, New York: Grossett & Dunlap, 1969.

[3]*Psychology Today,* December 1974, p. 60.

[4]Study by N. Rojas and A.F. Sanchi, *Archives of Legal Medicine, 11,* p. 29, 1941. Reported in *Natural Health, Sugar and the Criminal Mind* by J.I. Rodale, New York: Pyramid Books, 1968.

[5]Reported by Barbara Reed, Chief Probation Officer, Cayahoga Falls, Ohio, 1976.

[6]*Natural Health, Sugar and the Criminal Mind* by J.I. Rodale, New York: Pyramid Books, 1968; *Psychodietetics* by E. Cheraskin and W.M. Ringsdorf, New York: Stein & Day, 1974.

[7]Dick Gregory, from *Dick Gregory's Natural Diet for Folks Who Eat* edited by J. McGraw, New York: Harper & Row, 1974.

Chapter 12   Alienation

[1]From *The Yellow Emperor's Classic of Internal Medicine* edited and translated by Ilza Veith, Berkeley, Calif.: University of California Press, 1972.

[2]The universal teaching to eat according to season in the land in which you live is described in: Europe—*The School of Salernum: Regimen Sanitatis Salerni* translated by Sir John Harrington, Ente Provincial per il Turismo, Salerno, Italy 1975; America—The Mormon Word of Wisdom, *Doctrine and Covenants:* 89; Far East—*The Yellow Emperor's Classic of Internal Medicine;* Mid East—*The (Essene) Gospel of Peace* by E. Szekley, London: C.W. Daniel, 1973.
[3]16,000,000 pounds of chemicals—*Foodbook* by J. Trager.

[4]From *The Eater's Digest: The Consumer's Factbook of Food Additives* by M. Jacobson, New York: Doubleday, 1972.

[5]See *Why Your Children Are Hyperactive* by B. Feingold, New York: Random House, 1974; Food additives and hyperkinesis: a controlled double-blind experiment by G.K. Conners et al., *Pediatrics, 58,* 1976, pp. 154–168;

Food additives and hyperkinesis: A continuation study by C. Goyette and G.K. Conners, findings presented at American Psychological Association Convention, August 1977; Artificial colors and hyperactive behavior by J.M. Swanson and M. Kinsbourne, findings presented at American Psychological Association Convention, August 1978; A study of efficacy of the Feingold diet on hyperkinetic children by A. Brenner, *Clinical Pediatrics, 16,* 1977, p. 652.

[6]A test of the Feingold hypothesis: hyperactivity and food additives by J.P. Harley, C.G. Matthews, and P.L. Eichman, findings presented at American Psychological Association Convention, August 1977; challenge test of diet-responsive hyperkinetic children with artificial colors by C.H. Goyette and K. Conners, findings presented at American Psychological Association Convention, August 1978.

[7]Reported by Dr.A. Hoffer.

[8]*Human Ecology and Susceptibility to the Chemical Environment* by T. Randolph, Springfield, Ill.: Thomas, 1976.

[9]Underestimation of chronic toxicities of food additives and chemicals: The bias of phantom rule by S.H. Kon, *Medical Hypotheses, 4,* 1978, pp. 324–329.

[10]*Psychodietetics* by E. Cheraskin and W.M. Ringsdorf, New York: Stein & Day, 1974; *Psycho-nutrition* by C. Fredericks, New York: Grosset & Dunlap, 1976; *Mental and Elemental Nutrients* by C. Pfeiffer, New Canaan, Conn.: Keats, 1975.

[11]See *Human Dimensions,* Spring 1973, article by Sister M.J. Smith; *Prevention,* January 1974, article by J. Kinderlehrer.

[12]*Psychodietetics* by E. Cheraskin and W. Ringsdorf, New York: Stein & Day, 1974 (This book provides a nutrient-oriented discussion of the relationship between nutrition and behavior.).

[13]See *Composition of Foods* by B. Watts and A. Merrill, United States Department of Agriculture Handbook No. 8, U.S. Government Printing Office, Washington, D.C., 1975; *Nutritive Value of American Foods in Common Units,* United States Department of Agriculture Handbook No. 46S, U.S. Government Printing Office, Washington, D.C., 1976; *Nutrient Value of Some Consumer Foods,* Department of Health and Welfare, Govern-

ment of Canada, Ottawa, 1971; *Mineral Content of Foods* by Nutrilab, Inc., Haywood, California (n.d.)

[14]Some studies on the chemical transfer of learning: an experimental study of the chemical transfer of learning by ingestion by P. Jaya Kumar and I.S. Muhar, *Indian Journal of Psychology, 50,* 1975, pp. 215–221 (insects); Memory transfer through cannibalism in planaria by J.V. McConnell, *Journal of Neuropsychiatry, 3,* 1962, pp. 42–48; Memory transfer in rats by injection of brain and liver RNA, *Journal of Biological Psychology, 19,* 1977, pp. 4–9; Dose-dependent biochemical transfer of a classical conditioned effect by P.V. Laird, W.G. Brand, F. Saunders, & D. Shaefer, *Journal of Biological Psychology, 16,* 1974, pp. 3–5 (fish); Positive and negative transference of specific learning via injection of RNA extract in rats by B.W. Meeks, M. Merrill, & L.M. Cooper, *Journal of Biological Psychology, 15,* 1973, pp. 20–23.

[15]*Consumer Beware* by Beatrice Trumm Hunter, New York: Touchstone Books, 197__ (A comprehensive review of modern food production practices and their effects on health; well documented.).

[16]See *Nutrition Against Disease* by R.J. Williams, New York: Pitman, 1971; *Dietary Goals for the United States,* Select Committee on Nutrition and Human Needs (U.S. Senate), U.S. Government Printing Office, Washington, D.C., 1977; *The Book of Macrobiotics* by Michio Kushi, Tokyo, Japan: Japan Publications, 1977. Dr. F. Raucher former director of the National Cancer Institute and the International Conference on Cancer and the Environment (October 1977) have presented some interesting findings on this subject.

Chapter 13   Fat Foods, Milk Foods

[1]*Live Longer Now* by J.N. Leonard, J.L. Hofer, and N. Pritikin, New York: Grosset & Dunlap, 1974.

[2]Diet in coronary atherosclerosis by l. Morrison *J. American Medical Assoc., 173,* 1960, pp. 884–888; Mortality, arteriosclerotic disease and consumption of hydrogenated oils and fats by L.H. Thomas, *Brit. J. Prev. Soc. Med., 29,* 1975, p. 82; *Cancer: How to Prevent It & How to Help Your*

Doctor Fight It by G.E. Berkley, Englewood Cliffs, N.J.: Prentice-Hall, 1978.

[3]Cellularity of obese and nonobese by J. Hirsch and J. Knittle, *Fed. Proceeds., 29,* 1970, pp. 1516–1521; Cellular growth, nutrition and development by D.B. Cheek, J.E. Graystone, & M.S. Read, *Pediatrics, 45,* 1970, p. 315.

[4]Follow-up on physical growth in children who had excessive weight gain in the first six months of life by E.E. Eid, *Brit. Med. Journal, 1,* 1970, p. 74; Infant overfeeding by A.W. Meyers, *Nutrition Today, 9,* 1974, p. 36; Infantile overnutrition among artificially fed infants in the Sheffield region by L. Taitz, *Brit. Med. Journal, 1,* 1971, p. 315; Is breast-feeding best for babies?, article in *Consumer Reports,* March 1977.

[5]Milk foods have been linked to a wide variety of physical disorders; See *Human Milk and the Modern World* by D&E. Jelliffe, Oxford: Oxford University Press, 1978 (a comprehensive discussion); Milk Allergy by A.S. Goldman et al., *Pediatrics, 32,* 1963, p. 425; Milk allergy observations on incidence and symptoms of allergy to milk in allergic infants by K.D. Backman et. al., *Pediatrics, 20,* 1976, p. 400; Optimal infant nutrition: Avoiding allergies and other problems by Mary K. White, *LaLeche League Information Sheet,* Number 16, 1975 (bibliography containing abstracts of studies relating dairy food to allergies, intestinal and respiratory complaints); *Coping with Food Allergy* by C. Frazier, New York: Quadrangle, 1974 (a comprehensive discussion of milk allergy); *Nutrition Behavior and Change* by H. Gifft et al. Englewood Cliffs, N.J.: Prentice-Hall, 1972; Ulcerative colitis provoked by milk, S.C. Truelove, *Brit. Med. Journal, 1,* 1961, p. 154–165; *Food Is Your Best Medicine* by H. Bieler, New York: Random House, 1961 (Dr. Bieler also discusses the adverse effects of processed dairy foods on liver and endocrine function); see also *Milk,* Los Angeles, Calif.: G.O.M.F. Press, 1970; *Don't Drink Your Milk* by F. Oski and J.D. Bell, New York: Walden Books, 1970; interesting information has also been reported at the Conference of Quebec Association for Children with Learning Disabilities, March 1977, and by M. Kushi and Drs. M. Mandel, B. Jensen, and R. Bunai.

[6]From *Food and Man* by Miriam E. Lowenberg et al., New York: Wiley, 1968 p. 105.

[7]Reported by Michio Kushi, Boston, Mass, 1974. (M. Kushi is a

philosopher, teacher and author, founder of the East West Foundation and the Kushi Institute, Boston, Mass.).

[8]*Composition of Foods* by B. Watts and A. Merrill, United States Department of Agriculture Handbook No. 8, U.S. Government Printing Office, Washington, D.C., 1975.

[9]*The Book of Miso* by W. Shurtleff and A. Aoyogi, Brookline, Mass.: Autumn Press, 1975.

[10]*The Book of Tofu* by W. Shurtleff and A. Aoyogi, Brookline, Mass.: Autumn Press, 1976.

Chapter 14   Overeating and Obesity

[1]Maimonides as quoted by Moses ben Maimon.

[2]*Slim Chance in a Fat World* by R.B. Stuart & B Davis, Champaign, Ill.: Research Press, 1972.

[3]Manipulated time and eating behavior by S. Schacter and L.P. Gross, *J. Personality and Social Psychology, 10,* 1968, pp. 98–102 (many of Schacter's studies are reported in *Emotion, Obesity and Crime,* New York: Academic Press, 1971).

[4]Transformation of oral impulses in eating disorders: A conceptual approach by Hilda Bruch, *Psychiatric Quarterly, 35,* 1961, pp. 458–481; see also H. Bruch, *Eating Disorder, Obesity, Anorexia Nerosa and the Poison Within,* London: Routledge & Kegan Paul, 1974.

[5]*The Truth About Weight Control* by N. Solomon, New York: Stein & Day, 1971.

[6]*Nutrition and Your Mind* by G. Watson, New York: Harper & Row, 1962.

[7]In *Apharmacy Weekly,* Vol. 16, No. 23, 1977, it was reported that researchers at the University of Illinois Medical Center may be on the verge of developing a new "wonder drug," a chemically and biologically inert substance that could coat the lining of the stomach, instantly producing a temporary barrier, preventing the absorption of any food eaten. The drug

would allow one to eat what one wants and not gain weight—(an overeater's dream). The product has yet to be tested on humans.

[8]Article by W. Nolan in *Esquire,* 1973.

[9]*Proceedings of the Findings presented at the American Psychiatric Convention* symposium on acupuncture in psychiatry, 1975.

[10]A review of behavioral approaches to weight control by E.E. Abramson, *Behavior Research and Therapy,* 11, 1973, pp. 547–556.

[11]Behavioral treatment of obesity: the state of the art 1976 by R. Jeffery, R. Wing, & A. Stunkard, *Behavior Therapy, 9,* 1978, pp.189–99.

Chapter 15   How to Eat

[1]Effects of liquid and solid preloads on the eating behavior of obese and normal persons, cited in A Behavioral Approach to Control Overeating by E.G. Poser et al., *Proceedings of 5th World Congress of Psychiatry,* 1971.

Chapter 16   Sexual Disorders

[1]This list was comprised from a diverse collection of sources, both written and verbal.

[2]*Foodbook* by J. Trager, New York: Avon Books, 1972.

[3]From *Man's Food* by L. Jensen, Champaign, Ill.: Gerrard Press, 1953.

[4]From the psychology of the world of objects by E. Dichter in *Handbook of Consumer Motivation,* New York: McGraw Hill, 1964, pg. 66.

[5]Dr. Robert Mendelsohn, Nutrition and Cancer Conference, October 1978.

[6]*Consumer Beware* by Beatrice Trumm Hunter, New York: Touchstone Books, 1971.

[1]From Children with learning and behavioral disorders by A. Hoffer, *J. of Orthomolecular Psychiatry, 5,* 1977.

[2]Findings reported in *Food and Man* by M.E. Lowenberg et al., New York: Wiley, 1968 and *Nutrition Against Disease* by R.J. Williams, New York: Pitman, 1971; Early malnutrition as it relates to future learning disabilities by M. Winick, Conference of Quebec Association of Children with Learning Disabilities, March 1978.

[1]For reports of food related changes see *Nutrition and Your Mind* by G. Watson, New York: Harper & Row, 1972; *Psychodietetics* by E. Cheraskin and W.M. Ringsdorf, New York: Stein & Day, 1974; *Not All in the Mind* by R. MacKarness, London: Pan Books, 1976.

[2]From *Not All in the Mind* by R. MacKarness London: Pan Books, 1976.

[3]Dr. L.M. McEwen; his publications include: Enzyme potentiated hypersensitization: Five case reports of patients with acute food allergy, *Annals of Allergy, 35,* (2), 1975.

[4]*Hypoglycemia, Low Blood Sugar and You* by C. Fredericks and H. Goodman, New York: Grosset & Dunlap, 1969.

[5]J. Olney, *Science, 164,* 1969, p. 919 and *Science, 166,* 1969, p. 386.

[6] Michio Kushi, 1977.

[7]Beneficial effects of a high-carbohydrate, high-fiber diet on hypoglycemic diabetic men by T.A. Kiehm, J.W. Anderson, & K. Ward, *Am. J. of Clinical Nutrition, 29,* 1976, pp. 895–899; for more discussion of food allergy see *Coping with Food Allergy* by C. Frazier, New York: Quadangle, 1977, and *Dr. Mandel's Five Day Allergy Relief System* by M. Mandel, New York: Crowell, 1979.

Chapter 19 Raw or Cooked?

[1]From *The Story of Man* by C. Coon, Second, Revised Edition, New York: Knopf, 1962.

[2]See R. Hauschka in *Nutrition* on theories of Rudolph Steiner, London: Stuart and Watkins, 1967; Martinus literature, Martinus Institute, Copenhagen, Denmark.

[3]B.K.S. Iyengar, 1972.

Chapter 20 Attitudes When Cooking and Eating

[1]B. Snellgrove, London, England.

[2]Story of G. Oshawa.

[3]*East West Journal,* April 1977.

[4]From *Sugar Blues* by William Dufty, p. 160.

[5]Blood Pressure in Vegetarians by F. Sacks, B. Rosner and E. Kass, *American J. of Epidemiology,* 100, pp. 390–395.

[6]From *School of Salernum,* translated by Sir John Harrington.

[7]From *Time, Space and Man* by R. Braidwood and S. Tax, Chicago, Ill.: University of Chicago Press, 1946.

Chapter 21 Recommendations

[1]Self-selection of diet by newly-weaned infants by C.M. Davis, *Am. J. Dis. Children, 36,* 1928, pp. 561–579 (Infants allowed to select their own food thrived on a diet of their own choosing. [The study was carried out 50 years ago, no doubt the children were presented with less processed, "alien" foods than would be available today.])

[2]Findings presented on the symposium on Empirical Research on the Influence of Television Advertising on Children, *Psychological Association Convention,* August 1977.

[3]*Dietary Goals for the United States,* Select Committee on Nutrition and Human Needs (U.S. Senate), U.S. Government Printing Office, Washington, D.C., 1977.

[4]Ibid.

[5]Three recent sources reviewing the scientific findings on health and nutrition and setting out a dietary policy consistent with our own are: *Dietary Goals for the United States,* Select Committee on Nutrition and Human Needs (U.S. Senate), U.S. Government Printing Office, Washington, D.C., 1977; *Un Politique Quebecoise en Maitre de Nutrition,* Minister of Social Affairs, Province of Quebec, Canada, 1977; Longevity Center, Santa Barbara, California, described in *Live Longer Now* by J.N. Leonard, J.L. Hofer, & N. Pritikin, New York: Grosset & Dunlap, 1974 (Whereas none of the three describe the dynamics of sane eating [recommendation 2] they do advise: an increase in centered, "natural" foods; a decrease in extreme foods [sugar, sweets, coffee, meat, salt]; a reduction in fatty foods and avoidance of overeating.).

Index